Candlelight and Blessings: Symbols and Rituals for Death and Grieving

by Rev. Dr. David L. Bieniek

Pastor David,
Keep up the good
work!

Be Peace,
Rev. Dr.
Dave
Bieniek

APOCRYPHILE
PRESS

The Apocryphile Press
1700 Shattuck Ave. #81
Berkeley, CA 94709
www.apocryphile.org

Candlelight and Blessings: Symbols and Rituals for Death and Grieving

Copyright © 2017 Rev. Dr. David L. Bieniek
ISBN 978-1-944769-66-6
Printed in the United States of America

Dedication

This is for all of those who
taught me to care
Teachers in the classroom
and in the desks,
Teachers in the hospital
and on the beach,
Teachers in the living
as well as in the dying,
Friends, co-workers, family,
pets, and strangers,
And for the most important teachers
my mother, Dorothy, and
my husband, Ervin

Contents

"What do I say?" – Responding to Death as a Spiritual Caregiver

The chart said "Jewish" and armed with this knowledge and a comfortableness with Jewish beliefs, I knocked and went in. After a long and enjoyable conversation, I asked the patient if there was anything else I could do. The patient asked me to say a prayer, and as I mentally gathered my thoughts for a Jewish prayer, the patient pulled a large crucifix out from under her gown. I gave a little chuckle, and she asked "What?" I apologized and explained that her chart said "Jewish." "Jewish? I'm Catholic!"

"What do I say? I don't know how to deal with someone who is dying." Many times these words are uttered by friends and family faced with the death of a loved one or even a distant acquaintance. Yet, the reality is that most people will be faced with this reality, if they have not already.

Death is inevitable, mysterious, and often confusing. At the deathbed, patients and those gathered seek meaning, and many long for a sense of the Spiritual. Yet chaplains and spiritual caregivers have minimal information by which they can determine how to provide support, limited time to develop rapport, and varying expectations from those of the people they serve. This study was designed to identify symbols and rituals that are generally accessible and relevant across traditions, that vary in personal meaning, and that assist a dying patient in feeling grounded and aware of the Spiritual.

Chaplains and spiritual care providers are challenged to develop relationships with patients at or near death when, many times, the information provided to them on an intake form may be limited to a brief, often single word description of the patient's religious preference—usually a denominational attribution, a broad religious or spiritual category, or the ever-increasing "none." Similarly many communicate, "I am spiritual but not religious" when asked about a faith background. Most chaplains are familiar with the use of this strategy to dismiss them based on the patient's conception of what chaplains do and what services they can provide. Yet experienced chaplains seize this as the perfect opportunity to establish rapport and to connect.

A Pew Research Center poll finds that almost half of Americans believe they have had a "religious or mystical experience" and almost a third of those identify as having no particular religious affiliation.[1] It would seem, then, that mystical experiences are more common than some would expect. Although the definition for this poll was very broad, "a moment of sudden insight or awakening," the fact that people are recognizing and acknowledging these experiences is telling and helpful to those spiritual care providers who navigate the complex terrain of deeply personal conviction.

Popular media such as television shows and movies are packed with stories of ordinary people who have had extraordinary, mystical experiences, most attributed to some connection to the Spiritual[2]—ordinary people who do not consider themselves in any way to be religious. For example, television shows such as *Saving Grace* and *Joan of Arcadia* and movies like *Dogma* and *Michael* have storylines constructed in a similar pattern, ordinary people having visits from a spiritual being and, after that experience, they are led to make a difference in the world in which they live. Popular media is often a reflection of a constructed human reality. From this perspective it would seem that humans long for the connection to the Spiritual and seek that connection to make changes in their lives and the society in which they live.

These experiences are portrayed in media as a foundational realization that a mystical experience can transport the common person from simply being a creation in an ordinary world to actually having a part in the creation of an extraordinary one. Through a mystical experience with the Spiritual, the ordinary person becomes an extraordinary one and participates in changing the world through that experience.

These representations are broad religious interpretations. Mystical experiences, though common across traditions, are framed differently. In many religions, especially the Abrahamic religions, equating oneself with the Spiritual is a form of heresy. Yet when the mystic is brought into the mystical experience that is what happens.

Mystical experiences can be loosely defined as times when one feels as if the Spiritual is present, connected and united with the human, and the human feels a desire to effect a change because of this relationship. This union can take place in various ways and with various people and is often disconnected with knowledge or faith. Similarly, these experiences are independent of social standing, cross-cultural, and profoundly moving. As the Sufi mystics began explaining their experiences with the Spiritual, many were considered sinners. In an attempt to explain what was happening, Peter Awn writes of one Sufi mystic,

> For Abu Yazid and other ecstatic mystics, however, these expressions were simply ways to communicate their experience of mystical annihilation (*fana'*) in the Beloved. [3]

These mystical experiences intersect with moments when life has reached a crisis, like the death of a loved one, reach into the deeper spirituality, and connect those present to the Divine, regardless of how it is interpreted or defined. That is where we begin the exploration of symbol and ritual and their role in connecting the person in crisis to the deeper reality and in making the experience a life-affirming, spiritual time, even as one is facing death.

Operating off of this assumption that at some level all humans are spiritual beings, chaplains and spiritual care providers enter each engagement seeking to support each patient in a personally and culturally sensitive manner. Pierre Teilhard de Chardin is quoted as saying, "We are spiritual beings having a human experience."[4] This core of spirituality, the human experiences of life and death that are universally shared, is what unites people as a human family regardless of spiritual beliefs, race, creed, or economic status. As early as the 1930s, in a time between the World Wars, John Dewey suggested that humanity was getting away from a religion mindset into a "common faith of mankind [sic]" set in the values outside the confines of "sect, class or race."[5] This core of spiritual faith and practices can be broadly classified as "Common Spirituality."

This Common Spirituality is reflected in the symbols and rituals that many people and cultures, religions, and communities recognize for their deeper metaphorical and often mystical meanings. Many of these symbols are present in and foundational to rituals that might be recognizable by outsiders and nonmembers as familiar, shared experiences for them, though the meanings assigned to them may be somewhat incongruent.

These rituals and symbols become increasingly and profoundly more important at the end of life. Hospice chaplains and palliative spiritual caregivers can acknowledge and leverage these important symbols and rituals in helping loved ones say goodbye and giving the patient a peaceful exit from this life—a respectful death.

Regardless of the religious background of the patient and loved ones gathered at the deathbed, there are elements of symbol and ritual that take on a more pronounced role, and indeed even greater importance as one is facing the end of life. As chaplains physically enter the space where the patient is, they have the opportunity to assist the patient and gathered loved ones to transition from being closed off, isolated, and insular. Through making intentional and purposeful connections to the symbols and rituals at the deathbed, those gathered can more readily connect with their spirituality and open themselves to the realities of the death experience. It allows them to consider life beyond death, and a transformed relationship with the patient, who will continue to live in the hearts and minds of their loved ones, and in their shared memories and stories.

Yet, to provide this assistance, the provider must have knowledge of these symbols and rituals and a heightened awareness of their commonalities to many cultures and spiritual paths and the contexts in which they are used. These symbols and rituals function as a bridge between different religions and can empower chaplains with resources to enrich the end-of-life experiences for those they serve.

Practically speaking, "deathbed" means the time when the patient realizes death is inevitable, and she and her family and friends are preparing for her departure, or, in the case of nonresponsive patients, when those gathered come to that same realization. The continuum of care explored and expanded upon in this project is inclusive of the patient and family from the realization that death is near, through death, memorial service, and time of grieving. Each step of this journey is seen as a movement from, through, and beyond the deathbed, and ritual is incorporated all along the way.

This study seeks to explore these symbols and rituals that can be present at the deathbed, first examining common symbols and then exploring how these symbols are integrated into rituals that can be used to make connections at the deathbed by chaplains and other palliative spiritual care providers. In what ways can a minister, chaplain, or other caregiver use these symbols and rituals in a spiritual action that can help family members, friends, and the dying feel connected to the spiritual experience without excluding anyone from the experience?

Context of This Project

This study is conducted through the vocational and occupational perspectives of a board-certified hospice chaplain with experiences in a large urban area in central Texas as well as a rural island community in northwestern Washington. The experiences range from pediatric palliative care to hospice care with predominantly geriatric clients and all those in between.

Contextually the pediatric spiritual care experiences were primarily in a clinical hospital setting, whereas the hospice experiences were provided in home or out-of-hospital settings. Originally these hospice services were provided under a home health arrangement and subsequently as a self-contained program inclusive of the certification of the hospice. These contexts are important to the breadth of the study inasmuch as chaplains and palliative spiritual care providers are informed by organizational structure, community expectations, and overarching goals and mission. Hospice chaplains serve the spiritual needs of patients, family, and staff. At times that means just a one-time visit or phone call, but other patients may request more regular contact such as weekly visits.

This study was conducted by an ordained progressive Christian minister in Metropolitan Community Church, who is able to offer sacramental services to patients, family, and staff. Chaplains have been asked to provide baptisms, Communion, anointing, and funerals for patients—often across religious traditions. Religious and spiritual traditions vary in populations regionally in the United States. In the Pacific Northwest persons are more likely to claim "none" when asked about religious preference. This is reflected in national demographic data about religious affiliation by region.

It is an important contextual note that although many patients and family members are not interested in religion, they still often express a need for spiritual support and request services. They may not be interested in prayer or sacramental support, but they may need someone to hear their story, fears, and celebrations without any discussion of the afterlife, salvation, or other discourse that they perceive to be "churchy." Yet many express the desire for a spiritual discussion rooted in making meaning of their lives or their loved one's life. This may extend into a request for a blessing for themselves or their loved one as death approaches. They may desire a connection to the Spiritual, without giving it a name or proclaiming an expressed dogma or religious identity. Many patients and family members want to talk about death and mortality but may be reticent to bring the issue up to a person they have yet to know.

The context for this study has been framed in this particular population: people identifying a spiritual need, specific or ill-defined, yet pronounced and requested. This work of recognizing the symbols and rituals that can unite individuals regardless of any religious connection opens the possibility for a broader range of service and comfort. The question regarding symbols and rituals that connect individuals to the Spiritual - and how those can be used in the time of crisis - form the impetus for this study. For the context of this project, that time of crisis is the full continuum of the death process.

This full continuum extends to the period of bereavement. Often chaplains follow the families of deceased patients for a period of time—perhaps up to a year—providing support through mailings, visits, phone calls, an annual memorial service, and grief classes. Grief classes also provide a chance to use symbols and rituals to connect the grieving to the Spiritual. As such this study includes rituals that can be used in the grief and bereavement phases of the deathbed continuum.

Two Clarifications

As this work progressed there was specific attention and ongoing aware-ness of any semblance of cultural appropriation or lack of sensitivity to the cultural/religious symbols being explored and employed. Great care has been used in being sensitive and appropriate in use of symbols. The symbols are from a basic elemental place that is shared among many cultures and religions throughout human history. With this in mind, the chaplain feels that the symbols are used appropriately and sensitively and in the most inclusive sense possible.

The psychological dimensions a chaplain might face in walking into the room of a dying patient also present challenges and some-times concern. A chaplain might be faced with anger from the patient or family members, pain of past relationships with religion, or even denial of the dying process. This project is not designed to deal with these complicated issues and the chaplain is encouraged to deal with such situations sensitively and seek other professional assistance for the patient and family as necessary.

Toward a Common Vocabulary

Common vocabulary to describe the experiences at the deathbed is foundational to creating a framework that can be useful to chap-lains and palliative spiritual care providers. It was necessary to create operational definitions for terms that are used throughout this study. These operational definitions seek to create a level of accessibility for those providing spiritual care at the deathbed and are not intended to substitute for the personal beliefs of the patient or those gathered.

Throughout this project female pronouns have been used for patients and many family members. There are two reasons for this. The first reflects the reality that many of the patients included in this study who were visited and accepted spiritual care were female. Comparatively speaking, men access spiritual care visits with less frequency than women. This is also true of family members who accept spiritual care or bereavement care. Many times they are female.

The second reason for the use of the female pronouns is that, although the male pronoun is used often to mean the collective, i.e., either "male or female," it is an opportunistic praxis to use female pronouns to embrace the individualistic experiences at the deathbed.

In using pronouns for the chaplain, a decision was made to leave the pronouns male as that reflects the person who usually provided the service.

A Broader Definition of "Blessings"

Throughout the scope of this project as well as in the title, the word "blessing" is used. Though this word can connote religiosity, the term is used in a much broader sense: offering support, encouragement, and even permission. One might think of a young man asking for the blessing of the father of the woman he wishes to marry, a parent asking for a blessing on her children as she puts them to bed, or even the blessing of a boss as a worker leaves a job to pursue a new career.

Though these may seem like instances of one having power over another, they can be reframed as the mutuality of authority and the extension of communal relationship. Note that the blessings that are used and spoken of in this project are about giving life and connecting to the Spiritual in whatever sense that may have.

Expanding and Broadening the Concept of "the Spiritual"

This work is focused on a common, yet unique and deeply personal experience of the mystical at the time of death. Because terminology is easily misinterpreted or is usually approached with bias, it has been a great struggle determining what to call this mystic transcendent nature, the Presence that seems to unite people at this time regardless of religious beliefs or lack thereof.

In working to engage ritual and symbol to ease the suffering at the deathbed, those present often become aware of a deep Presence that is a unifying force—perhaps a common shared experience in the most humanistic perspective or a religious experience for others. For the purpose of this study, the term "the Spiritual" is used to encompass a collective and expansive experience, fully acknowledging that this is inherently limiting to the individual who may name this Presence by many other names—God, the Divine, the Sacred, the Goddess, Hashem, Allah, Anam Cara, Atman, the Buddha Nature, Peace, the Good, or simply Love. Engaging the Presence requires the chaplain to be present with the one being served and to approach that person in a manner that acknowledges the individual, a manner framed by the aggregate and informed experiences required of the spiritual provider, who is generally not from that individual's tradition.

It is important to note that although some people feel they have no connection to the Spiritual, it seems that all people seek to find a meaning for their lives and their relationships. This seeking is also a connection that is fundamentally part of the spiritual journey for many. Helping a person along that journey is also a role that a chaplain might fill, especially at the end of life of the person or loved one.

The Patient

In this study "patient" is used to identify the person who is the main receiver of the care being given. At times this patient may be unconscious, nonresponsive, or even dead, but regardless, the patient is the person who serves as the locus of care.

Beyond the Patient—Family, Family Members, Loved Ones

The terms "family," "family members," or "loved ones" describe anyone who has gathered around the patient and is not a member of a paid care team. Family members do not have to be related by blood or marriage as much as by affinity, love, or care. That being said, there are times when paid caregivers have become so integrated with the family that they too may be classified as "family members."

Chaplain

"Chaplain" is used to denote the spiritual care provider/leader involved in the death experience and may serve for the full continuum or for part of the experience. "Chaplain" in the most inclusive sense could describe a minister or clergy person, a palliative spiritual care provider, or even a friend who feels comfortable providing spiritual care.

Staff

Generally when the word "staff" is used, it can be any member of the paid care team—nurse, social worker, volunteer (though not technically paid), or aide.

Scope of This Project

This study includes a descriptive analysis of symbols and rituals and how they have been used to connect to the Spiritual throughout ages, cultures, and religions. This analysis includes the following: cross-cultural connections, variations in meaning, common spirituality/inclusive discourse, illustrations from practice, and limitations.

This analysis will then yield a more focused awareness and create an operational context that is a necessary step to move from gestures that could seem empty to the outside observer to a connection to the Spiritual for those involved and aware. The study seeks to classify common symbols and the rituals according to the four common natural elements of water, fire, earth, and air. The illustrations used in this study will be examples of specific rituals that can be used at the deathbed, after death, and during grieving. These have been developed as tools to be used by those who are ministering to the dying and grieving (see the broad definition of chaplain noted above). In a true sense humans can offer each other support, healing, and blessing, and these rituals attempt to illustrate ways anyone can offer these benefits.

Included in this study, in appendices 1 and 2, are resources that chaplains and other spiritual care providers may find particularly useful. The first is a compendium of blessings, prayers, and readings from various faith traditions and sources that can be used in conjunction with the rituals or alone. The second appendix is a list of musical elements that can be used at the deathbed or during funerals and memorial services. Appendices 3 and 4 are examples of specific rituals that can be used after a death and are explained in following chapters.

Chapter 1

Symbols, Rituals, and Awareness as Connections to the Spiritual

*"What were some of the things your grandmother liked to do?"
I asked as the family waited for me to pray at her deathbed. In
their stories I came to know a woman who used to love to dance
but had given it up once her husband had died many years before.
They told stories of how she loved to sew quilts, though she had
not been able to lately due to poor eyesight. In our prayer we com-
mended her to her husband's arms that they might dance through
eternity while she sewed a quilt of love and memories to wrap
around her family forever.*

At the deathbed, patients and those gathered with them often seek meaning in one of the most complex times in life. They often long for hope for recovery or extended time; others mourn the impending loss; and many express fear of what is next. Others draw on their religious traditions to inform both their hopes and their fears. The chaplain and spiritual caregivers at this time are called to be present yet unobtrusive, realistic without inducing fear, and understanding without claiming expertise in matters of personal faith. So, then, the chaplain returns to the question, in what ways can a minister, chaplain, or other caregiver use symbols and rituals in a spiritual action that can help family members, friends, and the dying feel connected to the Spiritual without excluding anyone from the experience? These will be introduced conceptually with a few illustrations and then explored in greater detail in chapter 3.

Symbols

First consider the role of symbols. Joseph Campbell offered, "A symbol... is an energy-evoking and -directing agent."[6] Paul Tillich believed that symbols' depth opened up the "dimension of reality itself."[7]

Symbols are objects that take on a deeper meaning for the person grasping them. Tillich also suggested, "Every symbol points beyond itself to a reality for which it stands."[8] And Louis-Marie Chauvet sees a symbol as different from a sign. "The distinction between 'sign' and 'symbol' turns according to us, on whether the subjects *as such* are taken into account (in a symbol) or not (in a sign)."[9]

Just as writing is made up of signs—lines and curves—that to the uneducated person may seem like scribble marks on a paper, tablet, or clay, it is only by deciphering those scribbles that the meaning of the symbols is revealed. In a much more personal and contextually relevant example, a linking object from a deceased loved one—a ring, a pendant, or a photograph—is a symbol of a love that has passed, whether from death or from physical or emotional separation. Those in the larger community, however, do not necessarily immediately recognize this symbol. Thus, questions might be asked: "Why do you wear that ring?" or "Who is that in the picture?" The symbol is both corporate and private, easily recognized but contextualized in the individual experience.

Some symbols are more widely recognized and may be misinterpreted relative to a person's individual experience with that symbol or what she perceives that symbol to mean. A cross worn around a neck or a fish symbol on the back of the car could signify the bearer of the symbol as a Christian, and other similarly aligned Christians might feel a camaraderie with the person. But another person who might have been hurt by the Christian church or who believes that Christianity has done more harm than good in the world (in the global or specific sense), might have negative feelings toward the symbol, and consequently, make broad generalizations about the person using it.

Many symbols require explanation, but the mere act of wearing something—a ring, a pendant, a cross or other religious symbol—elevates that meaning to the discerning observer. In essence, the logical conclusion is, "This is important to me, and thus I keep it close." These deeper meanings of symbol are worthy of study and expanded exploration. There are symbols in the world, used throughout history, that speak of a deeper sense, an inner meaning that humanity holds in common. Using a common elemental structure is a neutral and accessible way to unpack these symbols: water, fire, earth, and air. The elements cross historical, religious, communal, and sociological dimensions. These symbols will be explored in depth in chapter 2; however, it is important to frame and illustrate this concept using two readily available and relatable examples, water and fire.

Water has for many thousands of years been the symbol for life. Water sustains all life—human, plant, animals. Water is also used in daily life such as bathing and cleaning. And yet, as a symbol, water moves beyond practical application to metaphorical and often mystical significance. As Mircea Eliade suggested in a conversation of water as symbol,

> Consider that for many there seems to be a deeper meaning found in water - restoration, healing, rebirth. To state the case in brief, water symbolizes the whole of potentiality... Every contact with water implies regeneration...in magic rituals it heals and in funeral rites it assures rebirth after death.[10]

Many spiritualities use water as a symbol of spiritual cleansing, the healing of the internal spirit. Thus a running stream, gurgling brook, or waves on a seashore become in themselves healing elements.

Fire separates humans from other animals. It is commonly noted that it was the use of fire that moved humans into civilization. At a practical, functional level, fire has been used for warmth, defense, and cooking food. The practical gives way to the communal. As people gather around a fire, storytelling begins—the warmth and safety provided by fire creates the space for storytelling and preservation of an oral (or even written) history. It is a place of meeting and community.

Like water, metaphorical and mystical meanings are often attributed to fire. Across traditions and cultures, people use a single flame (or more) in ceremony and ritual. In speaking from her Wicca perspective, Deborah Lipp suggests:

> Fire can be a transformative force; in fire, the old is burned away and what comes out is utterly different... Transformation by fire is sudden and total.[11]

Whether it is a candlelight memorial for someone who has died or a stick of incense left to burn at a temple, the single flame becomes a place of memorial and reverence. Fire can transform a moment into a memory and darkness into light.

There are many other symbols connected to the other elements of air and earth as well as symbols that have a contextual or temporal meaning for the patient or family that will be explored. Some of these will be readily recognized by society, and others will have to have their symbolism explained. What is important is the meaning and the use of these symbols at the deathbed,

Consider the role that the chaplain plays at the deathbed in using these symbols. For depth of understanding, these symbols will be categorized as corporate/common and individual/relative. Both sets are important; however, the use of the symbol requires different entrance points by the chaplain or spiritual caregiver. Corporate/common symbols are readily accessible, content neutral, and meaning is individually assigned by the patient and those gathered at the deathbed. Chaplains and spiritual caregivers can introduce these to the deathbed continuum environment with minimal concern for offense, misinterpretation, or refusal. This is the type of symbol that Mircea Eliade might have been referring to in saying:

> The function of a symbol is precisely that of revealing a whole reality, inaccessible to other means of knowledge... The symbolism *adds* a new value to an object or an activity without any prejudice to its own immediate value.[12]

Individual/relative symbols, on the other hand, are personal and their meanings are less obvious, often idiosyncratic and less transferable to other patients. The chaplain's or spiritual caregiver's role in using these symbols is reversed. The chaplain creates the space and the invitation for the patient or those gathered to add these symbols to the deathbed environment and uses them to help create a sense of meaning and depth of connection. It is this type of symbol that Chauvet spoke of, saying, "Its symbolic power is due only to its connection with the other half," that is, the receiver of the symbol.[13]

Ritual

Symbols are often (though not always) tangible, representational, and passive; rituals, on the other hand, are active, responsive, and collective. Rituals, for the sake of this study, are considered to be a collective of actions. Rituals are, in a basic dimension, simple actions that have a deeper meaning to those who are enacting them. Catharine Bell connects symbols and rituals[14] in referring to Victor Turner, who saw symbols as the "smallest unit of ritual and therefore the smallest 'mechanism' of the transformation and integration effected in ritual.[15] Turner would continue this line of thought, saying:

> A ritual is a stereotyped sequence of activities involving gestures, words, and objects, performed in a sequestered place, and designed to influence preternatural entities or forces on behalf of the actors' goals and interests. Rituals may be seasonal, hallowing a culturally defined moment of change in the climatic cycle or the inauguration of an activity such as planting, harvesting, or moving from winter to summer pasture; or they may be contingent, held in response to an individual or collective crisis.[16]

Symbols are often used in rituals. Consider a commonplace, mundane example. The simple action of planting a tree has a routine—prepare the soil, dig the hole, place the tree, cover with soil, water, etc. This may not seem like much of a ritual, but when that planting is done in memory of someone who has died within a community that celebrates the life that has gone before, and the individuals participate in the planting, this simple act becomes a ritual, a ritual of remembrance. Rituals are active and may be rooted in tradition or they are active, built on the simple action and then assigned metaphorical significance. In her study of the uses of ritual, Bell attempts to separate ritual use from the need for social control or solidarity. Ritual is seen as a mechanism for meaning and transformation that can be separated from specific beliefs or belief systems.[17]

In *Creating Rituals*, Jim Clarke takes the normal course of life changes that we all face and creates a space for them to be sacred by use of ritual. Clarke offers what makes ritual and what makes ritual good. It is not simply about taking some element or action and repeating it with meaning, but it is about seeking the dark side of the ritual, looking for the deep meaning, engaging the community, and making use of liminal space and time. Clarke says, "Rituals are meant to be unique for each person, group, or situation... Ritual is always in the service of the participants."[18]

Using the same construct, corporate/common and individual/relative, the chaplain approaches rituals at the deathbed with similar skill—introducing ritual or receiving/brokering ritual all the while paying attention to the community that this ritual represents and the transformation that the ritual seeks to bring to the situation. Eliade speaks of this spiritual connection of ritual:

> [The person] does not lose himself, he does not forget his own existence, when he fulfills a myth or takes part in a ritual; quite the reverse; he finds himself and comes to understand himself, because those myths and rituals express cosmic realities which ultimately he is aware of as realities in his own being.[19]

This study seeks to illustrate examples of these rituals, exploring how they relate to the Common Spirituality and how they link people to each other and to that deeper reality we name God, the Spirit, Divine Presence, or Higher Power. This is not intentionally excluding atheists or agnostics in speaking of a Divine Presence, rather it is acknowledging the assigned meaning that the patient will make herself. Stanford University recently joined a growing list of colleges and military branches employing chaplains for their atheist, agnostic, and humanist students. Chaplain John Figdor expressed it this way, "Atheist, agnostic and humanist students suffer the same problems as religious students—deaths or illnesses in the family, questions about the meaning of life, etc."[20] We all experience the need for connection and an answer to life's spiritual needs—that life-emanating force that connects us all.

The Ritual of Storytelling

To illustrate this, consider the ritual of storytelling. This ritual is easily identified across cultures and tradition, is found in both the mundane and the spiritual, and is generally regarded as central to preserving memory and emotion. It is the active, reciprocal connection between storyteller and participant, informant and questioner. Whether it is the nighttime story ritual with a young child or the sharing of sacred scripture, storytelling has an ancient and immutable effect on the human condition. It connects one to the other—the past to the present to the future. Megan McKenna says, "The act of telling a story is a ritual. It seeks to transmit knowledge and pass on secrets of the heart and soul cherished by a community of people."[21]

All of the sacred scriptures that are shared among people are basically sets of stories that become a means of imparting history, knowledge, and/or lessons. Some of the earliest storytelling came from the Indus Valley and was eventually adopted as scripture by the Hindu religion. The Vedas were a series of stories that were retold for centuries of gods and goddesses and their great adventures in this world. They were meant to be oral tradition and may have existed as such for many centuries before being written down.

Similarly, the ancient Greeks created stories about their gods and goddesses to warn the humans of this time not to forget them and to remember the lessons taught through the epic tales. Other religions also had stories. The Norse myths are full tales of the gods and goddesses still being made into movies today (as are the Greek myths). Egyptian myths would inspire the building of temples and pyramids and long lines at King Tut exhibits.

The Jewish religion is full of written stories and wisdom from kings, judges, and prophets. Buddhists still tell the stories of their Enlightened One. Early Christians wrote several volumes about their founder Jesus. Mohammed is said to have written down the recitations (Qur'an) he heard in a cave. And Joseph Smith was said to have found and translated the Golden Tablets that became the Book of Mormon. Each of these examples is based on a common question—how does humankind seek to explain the unexplainable—the mystic experiences of humanity and the connectivity of spirit that unites us?

Storytelling goes beyond the written texts of great religions, however. It is common at gatherings of families and friends celebrating momentous life events to tell the stories of the loved ones gathered. Consider the significance of storytelling as a deathbed continuum ritual. Before death, family members recount the memories that mark a life. After death, wakes are specifically designed to allow the mourners to recount their favorite memories of the deceased as a way to celebrate and to remember the life that has passed. At celebrations of births it is common for parents and grandparents to tell stories from their childhood. And at wedding ceremonies stories are exchanged about the happy couple along with wishes of well-being for years to come.

Storytelling is an ancient method of celebrating in the human history. Cave drawings, masks, tapestries, and rock art all tell the stories of the people who had gone before. It was a way of telling and retelling the story so that it would be remembered and celebrated.

The ritual is in the telling of the story. It is through a simple act of telling a story that the community is joined together and life is celebrated. It is more than just a recitation of a history. There is a joining of members of a group as the ritual is reenacted, whether it is in a place of worship, gathered at a table, or gathered around a campfire on a foreboding summer's night. In chapter 3, we will explore the place that storytelling plays in the deathbed continuum and ways that chaplains and spiritual caregivers can leverage this ritual to bring comfort and solace in a time of tremendous emotion.

The Ritual of Sharing Food

One of the most common and universal rituals is that of sharing food or a meal. Somewhere along the way, many people learn that to sit and eat a meal together makes you a family. Food rituals are often varied by geography. For many growing up in the South of the United States, going to a friend's house often meant you were going to eat there. It just went without question; it was a sign of hospitality and reciprocity.

In that vein, the nomads of the Middle East who would give rise to the Jewish and Muslim religions, as well as other religions in that area of the world, knew the importance of hospitality. It was considered more than a breach of etiquette to refuse food, drink and shelter to a wandering person. It was considered a grievous act, as you might be dooming the person to death in the harsh desert environment. Instead you were expected to welcome the stranger, give them food and drink and allow them a place to rest. In short, you made this person temporarily part of your tribe. Thus began the belief that to sit with a person at a table made them part of your family. The person realized he or she was a welcome guest and afforded the comforts of home.

The mundane gives way to metaphor. It is not surprising, then, that the meal became an important ritual within its own right. Many religions incorporate a time of eating together as part of a ritual, if not the whole ritual. Meals became places and times of memorials, of remembering what had been done for the people in the past.

During Passover, the Jewish people celebrate God's deliverance of their ancestors from slavery in the land of Egypt. The meal is a symbolic representation of the story itself. The foods that are eaten all have symbolic meaning, and they help to tell the story of deliverance. And yet it is not just a retelling of the story. The meal and its symbolic elements are intended to be a reenactment of the escape. Parents are taught to tell their children, "This is what the Lord did for me as I was led out of Egypt."

In the Christian tradition, the Lord's Supper, also known as Communion, is meant as a commemoration of the last time that Jesus ate with his Disciples. It is generally believed that Jesus, a Jew by birth and upbringing, was celebrating the Passover meal with them.

Jesus on the night when he was betrayed took a loaf of bread, and when he had given thanks, he broke it and said, "This is my body that is for you. Do this in remembrance of me." In the same way he took the cup also, after supper, saying, "This cup is the new covenant in my blood. Do this, as often as you drink it, in remembrance of me."[22]

His actions have been interpreted widely throughout the 2,000 years since his death, but the central message is still that it is a commemorative meal that brings the believing Christian community into relationship with each other. As more Christian communities turn to "open Communion" where membership in that particular sect is not required, the family of those welcomed at the table is expanded.

The month-long fasting during Ramadan is ended each evening with a feast at sundown called the *itfar*. Again it is common to invite friends and strangers whom you have met to the daily fast-breaking meal. The entire month is concluded with a festival of great feasting called *Eid al-Fitr*. Again not only family and close friends are invited, but often this feast is open to the many friends, acquaintances, and others who have crossed the path of the family.

The reality is that meals become an important ritual in events around the globe. Birthdays, weddings, anniversaries, and even deaths are celebrated with a time when people gather to share food, drink, and stories. Seldom is there a time when human beings come together when food is not somehow involved. The question is, then, why is this so?

Perhaps it goes back to the main reason for humans banding together in the first place. Human beings are not that strong alone, but with combined resources, intelligence, and strength, humans learned they could bring down prey much bigger and stronger than they were. Once the prey was brought down, the logical next step was to eat together. They were possibly proud of their work. Perhaps they were also mourning the life of a comrade who did not make it through the battle. The young and the old who could not participate in the hunt were not excluded from the feast. Surely spirits were lifted and people enjoyed their time together.

This type of celebration continued throughout the eons even as we no longer had to hunt prey or even harvest our own fields. Humans found reasons to celebrate and those celebrations always seem to include food. Thus the meal became an important ritual that not only celebrated, but encouraged, community and common cause.

The sharing of a meal or food is often a significant deathbed ritual—from the connecting elements of favorite tastes to soothe the palette from the often bland and prescriptive dietary restrictions before death, to the giving and receiving of food in the post-death experience as a symbol of collective and communal caretaking. There are times when a family will have a final toast or share a favorite food item right after a death as a symbol and ritual of their love as well as their loss.

The Role of Awareness

Whether it is in the passive use of symbol or active involvement in ritual, those at the deathbed are called to a certain and attributable level of awareness. According to Merriam-Webster, awareness can be defined as

> The ability to perceive, to feel, or to be conscious of events, objects, thoughts, emotions, or sensory patterns. In this level of consciousness, sensory data can be confirmed by an observer without necessarily implying understanding. More broadly, it is the state or quality of being aware of something. In biological psychology, awareness is defined as a human's or an animal's perception and cognitive reaction to a condition or event.[23]

According to Jon Kabat-Zinn, another part of awareness is paying attention:

> Paying attention refines awareness, that feature of our being that along with language, distinguishes the potential of our species for learning and transformation, both individual and collective.[24]

From these definitions there are several pieces that can be explored and unpacked that will be helpful for future discussion of the use of symbol and ritual at the deathbed.

Awareness depends on sensory data, which is generally confirmed, but not always agreed upon. The senses that we have as human beings are an important part of our awareness. Awareness also depends on the understanding, bias, filter, and psychosocial affect of the perceiver. Thus many times the mystical experience can take on the social, political, and/or religious connotations in which it is encountered. Awareness is a function of the cognitive, affective, and spiritual domains that each individual brings to the deathbed experience.

Awareness as a function of cognition creates a necessary and often moral tension between emotional and intellectual understanding of an event—the struggle of heart and mind in the common vernacular. If a person is aware of an event at a cognitive level and simply pushes it out of her mind, then the full awareness does not take place. Awareness, for the sake of this study, is considered to be the intersection of the cognitive, affective, and spiritual responses to the deathbed experiences. Awareness, like ritual, is active. When the person speaks of the deathbed experience, writes about it, artistically expresses it, or even just quietly considers it, the event arises to the point of awareness. These criteria will be used in this study to describe, explain, and elaborate on how mystical experiences affect symbols and rituals at the deathbed.

Awareness then is rooted in the sensory perceptions but is highly influenced by the cultural, spiritual, and historical experiences of the perceiver. Awareness is the conscious perception of events that lead to a deeper understanding of its connection to other things. For the purposes of this study, that definition embodies the Spiritual.

Moving from the awareness of a mystical experience to how it might affect a patient and family's experience of rituals at a deathbed will require the chaplain or spiritual caregiver to take into account cultural/religious belief systems. The most demographically identified religions within the experience of the author (whether that be in study or in application in the clinical setting) are explored. The chaplain or spiritual caregiver cannot make generalizations based on religious affiliation, but is then challenged to create space at the deathbed that allows for awareness across and within tradition. This study seeks to identify those symbols and rituals broadly enough to allow for individual expression.

An illustration of awareness in both provider (chaplain or spiritual caregiver) and receiver (patient and those gathered at the deathbed) is relevant to frame the context of awareness for the rest of this study.

The Hindu religion is well known for its belief in reincarnation. The chaplain or spiritual caregiver not of the Hindu tradition must be aware in cognitive, affective, and spiritual domains of the context of this belief. Awareness involves understanding and compassion, not belief or compulsion. So, consider reincarnation. Many times reincarnation is misunderstood as simply a movement of the soul from one body to another, but, according to Kenneth Krammer, there are a variety of possibilities depending on how much unfinished *karma* needs to be completed. A soul can choose to be reincarnated, leave the physical dimension, or simply be absorbed into the ground of Brahman.[25] Thus Krammer goes on to say that as the Hindu approaches death there are several rituals to support the dying person including a few drops of water from the sacred river Ganges on the tongue, chanting, and readings from the *Vedas*. After death the body is cremated so the soul can begin its next journey.[26] Consider this personal experience in light of the corporate and decontextualized experiences at the deathbed where those exact symbols and rituals may not be present. The chaplain or spiritual caregiver is called upon to leverage accessible symbols and rituals to bring a level of heightened and familiar awareness to the deathbed.

Awareness in the Hindu traditions involves reciprocity. There is also a second mystical component of death in Hinduism whereby one meditates on anticipatory dying by meditating on his/her own death (while still very much alive) in order to free the soul and thus surrender to the Spiritual. Krammer says it is to be "dead to self, yet fully alive."[27] Deathbed rituals can create space for this to happen and allow participants to achieve full awareness in the cognitive, affective, and spiritual manners. Again, these rituals are not intended to replicate religious practice; they are intended to be broad enough to promote and allow for individual expressions of awareness.

A similar eastern tradition, Buddhism, has spread to many countries and cultures, and in each emanation of Buddhism it has successfully incorporated the cultural practices it encountered. Thus, it is sometimes difficult to apply specific death beliefs and practices to Buddhism. The Buddha taught that death was a dissolution of all the things that make up the self. The rebirth is not the same as in Hinduism, as the self has been dissolved, and yet rebirth might be necessary to continue the journey to Nirvana (enlightenment).[28] Death rituals are, then, about helping a person be ready to start the next part of the journey without fear or anxiety. It is also a common belief that the soul might wait for up to three days before it travels to the next state, so the body is prepared for cremation but is not moved or the soul might get confused.

Awareness in Judaism is similarly positioned, the collective of the cognitive, affective, and spiritual domains. The beliefs about death have changed and transformed, as well, and even today one will find a great deal of disagreement about what lies beyond death for the Jewish person. However, generally speaking the belief is that the soul and body are separated and both return whence they came—the soul to the Divine and the body to the ground.[29] Death rituals will include the dying person making a confession and reciting or hearing the *Sh'ma* and other prayers. If possible, the dying person should have the *Sh'ma* on the lips as death comes.[30] The body is not left unattended and is buried as quickly as possible, generally within twenty-four hours of death. In most Jewish cultures, cremation is not allowed. The death rituals continue after the death as the family sits *Shiva* for seven days and there is a yearlong period of official mourning for the family. The prayers, the symbols, and the rituals have specific form yet may be expressed to varying degrees by families with different levels of tradition.

Within Christianity, the beliefs around death revolve around the person's relationship with God - for some, that relationship at the point of death. Many Christians believe in a period of judgment right after death. After that, the immortal soul may enter Heaven, a place of eternal bliss with God, or be confined to Hell, a place of eternal torment without the presence of the Divine. Other Christians believe in an in-between place called Purgatory, where the soul is tormented for a period of time until it is cleansed, then released to Heaven. Some Christians have a belief that only a faith in Jesus Christ (founder/inspiration of the religion) as Lord and Savior is a requirement for Heaven; thus, it is reserved for faithful Christians. Conversely some Christians no longer profess a belief in Hell. Christian death practices vary, but most have some belief in the importance of confession of sins, profession of faith, and/or prayers and scripture reading. Some sacramental Christian sects have a particular ritual generally called Last Rites where a priest or minister uses holy oil and prayers to prepare the soul for leaving the body on its journey. After death, most Christian sects allow for cremation, though some still require the ashes to be buried. Generally there is no time limit between death and burial. As in other religions, fundamentalist and progressive components may interpret their tradition in different ways.

In Islam death is seen as a transition from this world to the next. In many ways the Muslim belief is similar to Christianity in that the soul is judged, and if weighed worthy, is allowed into Paradise. However there is a period of moving through seven layers of Heaven as the Day of Judgment is awaited, when the body is resurrected, and the soul is rejoined to the body.[31] In the Sufi branch of Islam, preparing for death is vitally important. This process begins with dying to oneself, which is best practiced while still living, so when death comes the believer will be ready.[32] The death rituals for Muslims include facing the dying toward Mecca, while the room is perfumed and unclean persons leave. *Suras* from the Qur'an are recited along with the basic creed of Islam, the *Shahada*. The dying person repents and if possible dies with the holy name *Allah* on the lips.[33] Awareness is highly personal, and the chaplain may find that awareness varies within the patient and those gathered. Breadth of expression allows for individual variation.

Beyond these five "main" religions, there are several others that the chaplain might encounter in ministry. A Chinese family of a Buddhist tradition was very opposed to touching their dying father and insisted that nurses and other caregivers wear gloves. The dying are never to be left alone and they should be dressed for their journey when they die. In this particular tradition the oldest son takes on the job of preparing the body after death. Having food at the bedside, especially citrus fruit, is important for the soul, and many deaths are accompanied with giving the dead money, tea, and sweets for the afterlife. Consider, then, the intersection of symbol and ritual as a function of awareness.

Earth-centered spiritualities and Pagan practices generally are centered on the awareness that the soul leaves this world and reenters the Cycle of Life, and most adherents believe in some sort of reincarnation. The body is simply seen as a vessel that is now empty as the soul leaves this realm and enters into the spiral dance of life. The body once again becomes part of Mother Earth to be reborn.

Awareness is foundational to ritual. Pagan rituals usually start with spiritual support during the dying process. The dying person is caressed, sung to, and allowed to discuss their fears and feelings about their passing. This is radically different from the way in which most modern Americans die, and is probably a lot closer to the way our ancestors dealt with death.[34] Commentary notwithstanding, Pagans wish to send their loved ones over to the next life knowing they are loved while embracing and releasing their fears.

Common to these various religious expressions (inclusive of the variety of individual expressions within them) are the following elements of awareness: recognition, evaluation, transition, and reclamation. Each component in this common spirituality at the deathbed is fully and specifically informed by the individuals involved. So the question remains: can a single ritual be broad enough to include both Hindu and Buddhist spirituality without claiming to be either? That is, then, the focus of this study and further exploration, and practical examples will be described in upcoming chapters.

People who are facing death with no identified spiritual support or with feelings of pain from past religious experiences may still seek out the comfort of the religion that they once knew. Awareness, then, is guided by the affective domain. In times of distress, humans may have a tendency to reach back for what they knew before. The comfort of the known is better than the fear of the unknown. So as a hospice chaplain, it is not unusual to hear a person ask for a Catholic priest, a Jewish rabbi, or a Buddhist monk, even if the patient has not been involved with that spiritual tradition for years. That mystical connection that the dying person may have found early in life may be the greatest source of comfort for them.

Others patients who have honestly felt no religious connection to any spiritual path still at times want to discuss spiritual things—awareness for them may be rooted in the cognitive domain. Troubling dreams, unfinished business with loved ones both living and dead, and wonderings about what will happen after death are all reasons that a chaplain might be called in to discuss with a patient who formerly declined a spiritual visit, claiming she was "not religious." For these, too, ritual connection is important, and the key is to find what type of ritual will help them connect with a spiritual experience.

There are times when a family member or patient requests a specific practice or ritual. Sometimes these are tied to a specific religion or culture. It is common for a chaplain to ask, "Close to the time of death, are there certain practices you would like for us to follow?" The family may not know right away, but may be open to hearing about these later.

Because awareness is an individual expression, the chaplain should be wary of overgeneralizing that a practice from one family or culture will apply broadly to all. The following illustration may serve to emphasize this point. In professional discourse, a chaplain learned from another chaplain that at the time of death Hindus prefer to be on the ground. As that was not possible in a hospital room, the care team lowered the bed as close to the ground as they could, and the patient's hand was actually able to touch the floor. Armed with this information, the next time the chaplain met a Hindu family whose loved one was close to death, he offered this for the patient. The family reacted with confusion. They had never heard of such a practice. This lesson then is critical to this study: the chaplain must approach the deathbed experience with breadth and invite depth, for to assume a belief is practiced across an identified culture is often a misinterpretation.

With all of this in mind, the question here is to how to give patients and family members a connection with the Spiritual, an experience of spiritual presence, a union with a larger reality that can be identified as a mystical experience regardless of what their or the spiritual caregiver's religious background might be. Are there elements and rituals that can be used in most cases that will help the dying feel a connection to something that is larger than themselves and their life? The further exploration of basic symbols and rituals that can connect one to another as well as to the Spiritual will afford the provider a resource that will allow receivers to find meaning and connection at the deathbed continuum. This study will explore some of these symbols and rituals and the author will make some suggestions on how this Common Spirituality can be used across traditions by illustrating some of the ways that rituals and symbols have been used at the deathbed continuum in a broad, inclusive, and relative manner: before and at the moment of death, in memorial services, and in the bereavement time that follows.

CHAPTER

2

A Beginning Organizer for Symbol and Ritual: The Four Elements

He still greets me many Sunday's holding out his rock in his outstretched hand. After several years the rock he received from our grief group still provides him with support and encouragement.

When looking for an organizing structure for symbol and ritual, one needs look no further than the basic elements of water, fire, earth, and air. These elements have spiritual, cultural, and metaphorical meaning across spiritualities, ancient and new. Because they represent the foundational elements of human existence, they are less susceptible to singular adoption or claims. Conversely, they are universal, common, and highly regarded across tradition.

Chaplains encounter many people of many different faith backgrounds and spiritual traditions. As such, many chaplains devote time and energy to the extended study of world religions. In the training of chaplains and healthcare workers, it is important to encourage those entering the field to engage in receptive conversations with patients about the patient's spiritual path, to ask patients about their religion if it is unfamiliar to the caregiver, and never to assume knowledge of how someone observes or adheres to their religion or spiritual path.

For many, this spiritual curiosity stems from academic World Religions classes, from experiences with friends of different traditions, and from those times when unintentional mistakes were made in overgeneralizations. For others, this is what really lights an interest to discover how other people connect with the Spiritual. Perhaps this is the core of chaplaincy—spiritual curiosity, the willingness to be open, and the resistance to impose a personal belief system on others. But more importantly, it is, perhaps, a driving need to discover how we can connect with each other—what are the common points that we celebrate? Starting with these basic elements, the chaplain can create a sense of connection and provide an opportunity for the patient and those gathered to assign their own personal and corporate meanings. In this chapter, the four basic elements will be explored in the broadest introductory sense and will be elaborated upon in upcoming chapters with more specific context.

Water

One of the most foundational and fundamental symbols found across traditions is water. From the earliest times, water was an important symbol and, for many cultures, a spiritual touchstone. Most ancient generations talked about the sacredness of water—perhaps from a purely functional perspective or perhaps for the deep symbolism water inspires. Many traditions embrace the importance of water in the act of bathing as a ritualistic cleansing or in the use of water as welcoming to community. Shinto young men bathing in the waterfall, though the water was obviously freezing, is a vivid and significant image. The Buddha found enlightenment sitting next to a river. Taoists talk about the importance of allowing the energy to flow like water, that which is sacred. Hindus still bath in the sacred River Ganges. The Zoroastrians see water as one of the sacred elements. The Jains remind us of living beings in all the aspects of life, including water. And Jews, Christians, and Muslims (like the Shinto) all have sacred cleansing rituals that are important to perform. Though most Christians are only baptized once, many use Holy Water throughout a liturgical year to remind them of the promises made by or for them.

In considering symbols and related rituals at the deathbed, one could first consider water, for water is a relevant and present symbol that seems to be related to the pure essence of life and existence—both physical and spiritual. Water is there at conception, at birth, and throughout people's lives, and many times is involved in the last ritual loved ones will perform by bathing the body after death. So as chaplains and spiritual caregivers explore symbols and rituals within Common Spirituality, they are often secure in the universality of water as a common and sacred symbol. The application of water symbols and ritual will be illustrated in upcoming chapters.

Fire

Fire is a significant symbol for many reasons. Generally considered, it illuminates; it warms; it consumes. Fire brings light to the darkest night and warmth to the coldest day. Fire, like water, is used across spiritual traditions and is a foundational symbol that, when viewed in and of itself, is content neutral; however, it is often assigned symbolic significance by those seeking that meaning.

But in terms of symbol and ritual, fire is used in many sacred rites from lighting a candle at a Christian Baptism to the Hindu funeral pyre. Spiritual people light candles for prayers, in memory and memorial, and as symbols of hope and light in times of crisis and fear.

At the deathbed, there are many ways that fire can be incorporated. As in any care environment, caution should be exercised, especially if oxygen is being used. Lighting a candle or several candles in memory or as a way of focusing prayer, hope, and/or grief is an effective way to bring a sense of spiritual connection to the patient and those gathered. For some, fire might be used to light incense or sage, which allows the patient and those gathered to remember that prayers and supplications go upward and into the realm of the Spiritual. Even a light left on in a darkened room can be a comfort for a patient or a signal of where the button is to get help, which becomes symbolic of fire as an element of both comfort and safety. Common to many, fire is still a specific representational symbolic element. As such, variations of fire symbols will be included in the sample rituals described later in this study.

Earth

Whereas water and fire have broad and expansive symbolism across traditions, earth is a bit more obtuse but nonetheless relevant and germane to this conversation for chaplains and palliative spiritual care providers. Earth is the place where things are planted. Earth is the grounding and the place of new life. Earth as a sacred symbol across traditions is the manifestation of meaning making and relevance most specifically connected to the beginning of life and the ending/beginning found in death.

The earth has been a sacred place from the beginning of time. Most spiritualities hold to the belief that humans originated from clay molded and brought to life either metaphorically or literally. Earth, especially fields, are regarded as sacred and to be appeased so it will give life to plants that in turn feed humans. Earth for some is the place where the dead are buried and then remembered or forgotten.

Mountains, deserts, and forest cathedrals become places to go for healing, meditation, and deeper connection with the Spiritual. Whether it was prophets who climbed mountains to hear wisdom, ancient mystics who went to the desert to find the Spiritual, or modern hikers who go out on long hikes to find themselves, the earth has always been a place of ritual and symbol.

Power and importance have been attributed to rocks and stones. Eliade suggested:

> Men [sic] have always adored stones simply in as much as they represent something *other* than themselves. They adored stones or used them as instruments of spiritual actions, as centres of energy designed to defend them or their dead.[35]

Megaliths, stone circles, Ebenezer stones, altars, and tombstones all speak to the power of stones in human history. And yet small stones are also found to have power. Carved figurines and other stones have been found in burial sites and holy places.

Stones can also be used in modern-day rituals, and one such ritual is described in chapter 4. This symbol and accompanying rituals are generally better suited to the grieving phases of the deathbed continuum and may not be as readily identified as personally and spiritually relevant at the time of death unless specifically noted by the patient or those gathered.

Air

At the deathbed, air is manifest in oxygen tubes, respirators, and other devices. Without air, life ceases to exist. This is brought into even greater meaning and more foundational significance as chaplains help families and loved ones participate in the patient's last breath. At the deathbed the seasoned professional is aware of the change in breathing and final expulsion of air. But this reality is transitional in the deathbed continuum. Consider the role that air, in the form of breathing or breath work, plays prior to that time. Breathing is the best example of symbol and ritual that uses this element. Common to most basic meditations is to sit and focus on the air filling the lungs and then exiting through the nostrils. Whether done in a group or individually, focusing on the movement of the air into and through the body becomes a sacred spiritual act.

Wind has often been seen and experienced as the movement of the Spiritual through the world. Most spiritualities have a belief that it is through the wind moving in the world that the sacred elements also move. The wind is symbol of communion with the Spiritual.

Air also makes sound possible. The chanting voices, singing choirs, and even ringing gongs would be nothing without the element of air to make those rituals strong and true. The Jewel Mantra is a widely used chant that is recited by Buddhists and Hindus around the world. This sacred use of air brings peace and well-being to the chanters and those hearing it. The wording for the mantra can be found in Appendix 1, "Mantra of Avalokiteshiva."

Air in breathing exercises and meditations, in chimes and wind, in chants and song is a foundational symbol that can be broadly presented and specifically requested. Again these are explored in greater depth and illustrated in later chapters.

A Word about the Ultimate Sacredness of All Elements

Each element can be considered in isolation or as a part of a collective whole. Because most spiritual and cultural traditions include these, the chaplain is sufficiently prepared to offer these as symbols of comfort at the deathbed. As with all symbols, meaning is assigned by the patient and those gathered. Chaplains should avoid assigning meaning to these symbols.

The breadth and interrelationships of these elements is elaborated on by some traditions. The Zoroastrians have a deep belief in the sacredness of all of these elements. This sacredness is so much a part of their teaching around life that, according to strict Zoroastrian code, none of these elements are permitted to be used in disposing of an empty body, a corpse, the ultimate in defilement. Bodies are not buried, burned, or disposed of at sea. Instead the ancient practice, still in use in many places, is to place the body in a tower and allow nature to take its course. This usually involves vultures and other scavengers, though more recently solar panels have been used to focus the sun's rays on the body and enhance decomposition.

Wicca, Native religions, and many earth-based spiritualities see the elements not as symbols or part of a ritual, but as actual sacred manifestations themselves. Thus the earth, the rain, the wind, and the sun are not simply elements of the Spiritual, but are the Spiritual. And consequently, dances, sacrifices, and other sacred movements are made to appeal or to appease the elements. Though the rituals may use these elements, it is to remind those present of the Spirit that abides in them.

The sun, moon, and stars; great rivers, such as the Ganges, the Nile, and the Amazon; ancient mountains and volcanoes; and monsoons, cyclones, and tornadoes were not just seen as manifestations of the Spiritual but were/are worshipped as gods and goddesses. Rituals surround the worship of these elements that often involve these elements themselves, as well as human actions. Ancient Celts and neo-Pagans light bonfires on the Winter Solstice to encourage the return of the sun. Hindus still bathe in the River Ganges as the birthplace of all life.

From the Wicca tradition, this thought seems to operate among all spiritualities concerning symbols and rituals.

> The miracles of nature around us inspired the birth of magic. These same processes sustain our lives…nothing separates them; they are one… These symbols, in and of themselves, possess little energy. They must be created (by physical or visualized means) with personal power. Only then will they focus and transmit energy [blessing].[36]

The importance in any symbol and ritual is not the innate magic, but the power that is given to these actions by the community. This book will now shift the focus to using these symbols and rituals in specifically aiding the dying and the grieving to connect to the Spiritual.

3

Uses of Symbol and Ritual at the Deathbed

I walked into a living room with a beautiful view of trees, water, and mountains. The hospital bed was surrounded by stacks of poetry books. "Pick up a book and open it to a poem and read it to me. It's what I do for all my visitors. Helps to break the ice." For the next hour our conversation wrapped around his impending death and the journey he was taking but was inspired by "Mussels" by Mary Oliver.

C onsidering the four elements as foundational to symbol and ritual across traditions, the chaplain or palliative spiritual care provider can use these to create a personally meaningful context for the patient and her family at a time when they may be preparing for her death. In order to prepare for the use of symbol and ritual at the deathbed, the chaplain must understand the relevance of the symbol, avoid assigning personal meaning, and invite the patient and those gathered to participate.

Additional Symbols and
Common Rituals on the Deathbed Continuum

This study seeks to present symbols that have cross-cultural connections, may have variations in meaning, are connected to the Common
Spirituality associated with them, provide relevant illustrations, and
discuss limitations. The illustrations will be expanded upon in Chapter 5.

Spiritual Elements

What follows are several elements that might be used in a bedside
ritual. They are placed in a category together in recognition that they
are spiritual elements in many different religions and spiritual paths.
This by no means requires their religious significance to be used in a
ritual. Some of these symbols are elevated to the level of symbol by the
assignation of meaning by those involved.

Candles

Connecting to the discussion of the four elements, candles represent fire
and are generally and broadly used. A single flame of a candle is used as
a sign of a memorial or a sign of hope. Many religions used candles or
open flames in rituals as a reminder of the "divine spark" or the flame
of life within each person. When speaking of rituals at the deathbed or
in a hospital setting, one must consider whether oxygen is being used.
If so, an open flame cannot be incorporated. However, there are many
electronic possibilities available and some have the aroma of real candles.

Artifacts

Many people find comfort in statues, pictures, or other sacred elements
and may have these available at their bedside. It is important to acknowledge the presence of these items to the patient or to the family members
present. If it is someone or something unfamiliar to the chaplain, he
should ask about it. If it is important enough to be there, the person

will be interested in telling the history and reason. If possible, and if it is comfortable, somehow incorporate these items in the ritual.

Sounds (Spiritual Musical Elements)

Sound is an elemental representation of air. This is a separate category from music. This instance refers to bells, singing bowls, chimes, or other such elements that may have a special significance to the dying. Many times a single chime or bell can lead to a deeper sense of the Spiritual that is present. It can be done to begin a time of reflection as well as to end it. A chime can also be used to represent many individuals, for example, chiming the bell once for each person lost in a tragedy. It is also important not to overuse such an element. One time a bowl was rung 108 times (a sacred number in Buddhism) during a World AIDS Day Service. Such overuse can become difficult for those present.

Breathing Exercises

Breathing is also a manifestation of the element air. If the dying person is still able to be cognizant of her breathing, ask for her permission to walk her through a brief meditation to help her feel more at ease and to focus on a deeper connection. Encourage the patient and all those present to focus on the breathing and to take in as deep a breath as possible without causing distress or pain. As they breathe, remind them that breathing is what unites all living things and that even plants and bacteria breathe. Remind them that in breathing they bring in what it is bodies need (oxygen) and get rid of that which bodies do not need (carbon dioxide and other impurities).

Explain that those present can also use this breathing to bring in what our spirits need. Lead them gently on a breathing meditation wherein as they breathe in air they also imagine that they are breathing in various good things that are needed for spirits to be at peace— light, energy, peace, goodness, compassion, love, hope, strength, etc. As they exhale encourage them to dispel (get rid of) those things that are holding their spirits back—darkness, tiredness, anxiety, worry, anger, hate, fear, weakness, etc.

Encourage them to concentrate on this breathing in and out for several minutes. Then tell them that they can come back to this simple meditation any time they need to, and to imagine each time that they are breathing in the good and breathing out the problems. Also remind them that each time they use this method, know that all of their loved ones are also breathing with them and in fact all of creation is breathing with them. They are connected to all that is living. This breathing exercise is used in rituals that follow in the next chapter.

Scents, Incense, and Holy Smoke

Many spiritualities use various scents and sacred smoke to honor the presence of the Spiritual. Incense and burning sage are just two examples. With adequate ventilation and explanation, these elements can be very calming and centering to the dying, especially if they have had some connection to the scent before.

A Catholic might find a great deal of comfort smelling the scent of frankincense, while burning sage might remind a Native American patient of the times they have been smudged to ward off evil and prepare for a new adventure. As with candles, this element may not be appropriate in all settings, especially where oxygen is in use or smoke detectors could be set off. Again the simple scent of elements may be potent enough to conjure memories and comfort.

Water

Water is elemental and used as a source of ritual cleansing in many different religions. Whether it is the Baptism of Christians, ritual cleansing in the *mikveh* of Judaism, bathing in the sacred River Ganges for Hindus, or the sacred waters of Shinto, water becomes an important part of many spiritual paths.

In many Christian churches water is offered for any believers to dip their hand in and water is sprinkled at various times in a service—reminders of the Baptismal promise made or renewed by the believers. The same ritual can be repeated for the individual on the deathbed simply by making the sign of the cross on the forehead.

Likewise, a small vial of water from a sacred river or pool can be kept near the dying person as a reminder to them of the closeness of that sacred place, even if they cannot be there at the present time. A single drop of water from the River Ganges on the tongue of a Hindu patient may be an important connection to the patient or family.

The sound of running water, such as a stream, is found to be a deep symbol of healing. In the room of a dying person, the sound of a gentle fountain might be soothing and a connection of that deep healing that can come from water gently cleansing us from the inside out.

Water is also important in quenching the parched lips and mouth of the patient, reminding them that as the water (or ice chips) can quell their thirst, the same water can be refreshing to the spirit. Water is life, and even the patient who has chosen to forgo artificial hydration can still have her lips and mouth kept damp to refresh body and soul.

Oil

Oil has often been used in the anointing of kings and of babies as a symbol of blessing, wisdom, and renewal of purpose. Anointing of the sick was practiced in the Greek world as well as early Jewish culture. This anointing was later claimed for Christian use by James the Apostle and brother of Jesus. Since then it has become a sacrament in Roman Catholic, Eastern Orthodox, and some other Christian denominations.

Though this anointing may not be accepted by all individuals, it is something that can be offered that may bring comfort. The anointing does not have to follow a particular form or even a particular religious blessing. The anointing can simply be a sign for healing of mind, body, and spirit. Using a simply worded blessing as the forehead is anointed can bring strength to the patient. A sample of such a blessing will follow in one of the rituals offered in the next chapter.

Sacred Readings

There are many readings that can be used at the bedside near the time of death. Almost every spiritual tradition has a prayer or reading that is appropriate at the time of death, and there are several books that can help to identify those readings or prayers. Appendix 1 will list sample prayers that have been used, and the chaplain will be able to access books that have collections of prayers.

Though some of these prayers are for specific religions, many of them can be adjusted for use in nonreligious practices. Many times the word "God" can be substituted with "Peace" or "Love" without losing the meaning. Some of these prayers listed in Appendix 1 avoid religious language altogether.

The 23rd Psalm is often included in rituals for Christian or Jewish patients. This is perhaps the best known of any of the Psalms and perhaps the best known scripture from the Judeo-Christian Bible. It is accepted by Christians and Jews as sacred scripture, but it is also widely accepted by the general public as an appropriate reading at the time of death. Though it invokes the "Lord," its appeal seems to go beyond a prayer. The images of being led through the darkness and into a garden and a lush banquet, protected from harm, allow the dying and those present to feel solace.

One author has taken the 23rd Psalm and has rewritten it in language that replaces "the Lord" with "Beloved."[37] Bobby McFerrin replaced the masculine imagery with female imagery as he rewrote the psalm in honor of his mother.[38] There are also many sung versions of the psalm that are also appropriate for use at the bedside.

There are also many secular readings that are appropriate for use at the deathbed. Several of these have been listed already and others will be noted later in the project, but two authors who were commonly used in rituals are Mary Oliver and John O'Donohue. Mary Oliver has several poems that the chaplain can keep on hand to use, especially "In Blackwater Woods," "When Death Comes," and "Wild Geese." John O'Donohue was a Celtic author, whose blessings, "On the Death of the Beloved," "For Absence," and "Entering Death," as well as many others from his *To Bless the Space Between Us,*[39] speak to the human heart at various times of need. Appendix 1 lists these and other readings from these authors.

Spiritual writings do not have to be from a sacred book. It is the guidance that these writings give to the life that is lived that make and keep them sacred. One patient loved reciting "The Cremation of Sam Magee" by Robert Service from memory even though she had advanced age and dementia. Her family requested that this poem, which is usually recited around campfires, be incorporated in her funeral. The patient's love of this poem made it cherished memory for her family and friends. It brought laughter and happy memories to those present.

Personal Symbols

Often a patient has personal symbols that may be included in the ritual. At the bedside, the chaplain may simply ask the patient or family if there is something that has special meaning for them either in the room or nearby. Often there is a poem or piece of writing that might be present at the bedside or hung on the wall somewhere easy to read. These have significance to the person and can easily be incorporated in a bedside ritual.

As an example, one patient had a copy of "Desiderata" hanging in her bathroom and, when asked about it, she said it was her guiding principle, her only religion. She wanted it read at her funeral. The chaplain was able to incorporate many parts of it over the next visits. Another patient had a copy of "Children Learn What They Live" as her guiding principles.

Music

In the same way that sacred writings can be incorporated, so can music. There is a growing body of research that suggests patients with severe dementia can still respond to music.[40] For many people, music is a connection to memories and happy times. Incorporating music into a bedside ritual helps the patient and family connect to a deeper spiritual realm.

If the patient has a particular religious background, then using pertinent religious music as a method of ritual is warranted. Christian hymns can be sung or played and a favorite of many is "Amazing Grace." For Jewish patients singing the "*Shema*" or the "*Mi Shebeirach*" may help them feel at ease. Chanting has long been a method of healing for Hindu and Buddhist patients.

If the patient is a veteran or has a strong national identity, using the national anthem of their country or other nationalistic hymns may bring meaningful memories. Many patients who were born in foreign lands hold these songs as important and connect them to happy memories at the time of death. However, be aware that not all veterans would find these songs helpful and not all immigrants want to be reminded of the homeland they might have escaped. Always check out the assumptions and seek guidance from the patient and those gathered.

The patient herself may have songs that she or family can identify as important for her own spiritual journey. Playing these songs during the ritual is warranted and encouraged. One patient had selected "Sissy's Song" by Alan Jackson as her gift to her family and had it played often. There is a list of such songs in Appendix 2. But chaplains are encouraged to speak to the family and, if possible, to the patient for suggestions on which songs or types of music to include. There is a wealth of knowledge to be gained by simply asking what is important.

Many families will have some sort of music playing for the loved one as they wait for death. Many times this will simply be quiet music to create a sense of calm.

Stringed instruments—violin, cello, and harp especially—have a way of calming the spirits around them as they are played. Whether the music is live or recorded, the benefit can be felt. A chaplain remembers a time walking into what was usually a very chaotic floor of the hospital. At first the chaplain noticed the lack of chaos. People were walking instead of rushing and there was an ease on the floor. Then the chaplain heard the beautiful music of a violin wafting through the air. One of the dying patients on the floor was a violin teacher and one of his students had come simply to play for him. Rather than closing the door, the nurses had left the door open so that the beautiful music was present to everyone on the floor. The student's gift was well received not only by the patient but by everyone on that floor that day.

Photographs

Photographs are powerful visual symbols and are often ways the chaplain can build rapport and determine the ritual appropriate for the family. Photographs will sometimes be a part of the memory and storytelling. Many times photographs of the patient as a stronger, healthier person help a family remember the patient before the illness. Sometimes families are encouraged to bring such photographs to hospital rooms and hospice beds. The family can also use these photographs at funerals, especially if it is a closed casket or cremation, to remind loved ones that this one who is dead can still live in memories of happier, healthier days.

Photographs of special places and events—vacations, marriages, births—are all very important in the history of a family. Incorporate these in bedside rituals as well. Being able to ask a patient or family member about why this particular picture is important gives the chaplain an opening to a whole new set of stories and memories. The photographs become another way that symbol is incorporated.

Art Pieces Created by or for the Patient

At times there will be art pieces—paintings, ceramics, quilts, etc.—that are present at the bedside. Recognizing these and again incorporating them into the ritual gives credence to the maker of the object as well as the gift itself. If the patient created the pieces, reminding the family that they are gifts the patient leaves them, and that they will be a way that the patient will continue to be with them for many years, might bring comfort. If it is an art-form or medium the patient has not been able to do for some time, recognizing that the spirit of the loved one will soon be freed and will be able to do this again in some sense can also bring comfort. For instance, the grandchildren of a quilter will now be able to sense grandmother in the reality of her quilt but also in the sense of the quilt of love she continues to wrap around them.

Nature

Having natural elements present is not always possible, especially in some hospital rooms. But it seems that having natural elements lends a deeper connection to the ritual. The natural elements might be flowers or a plant in the room. It might simply mean having a window shade open to see trees or sunlight outside. In the rare cases when the patient can actually be outside or on a deck or patio, use this for advantage to connect the loved one to the wider world. If the patient had a particular love—gardening, backpacking, skiing, etc.—recognize that in your ritual as well.

Recently a former forest ranger on hospice care wished to go into the woods one last time. The hospice nurse, chaplain, and the team, with the support of the local EMS, took the patient on a gurney into a nearby woods. In this final ritual, the ranger was able to feel once again the natural cathedral around him. [41]

For many spiritualities, connection to the natural world is seen as vital to the religion. Native American religions and Wicca/Pagan religions see the natural world in cycles, and life and death are also parts of that cycle. As gently as the seasons transition from one to the other, so too do our lives rejoin this cycle of birth, death, and rebirth. Using this natural connection regardless of the spiritual background of those present can help the loved ones feel a connection to the sacredness of the occasion.

Sacred Touch

It is ironic that many family members gathered around the bed of a loved one may be afraid to touch the patient. Yet from the moment humans are born until the moment they die, most crave and even need touch. Encouraging loved ones gathered at the deathbed that it is all right to touch, stroke, and even kiss the dying person is appropriate and important, all the time respecting personal boundaries and fears. Some simply need permission though.

Before the ritual the chaplain may take the hand of the patient and speak the patient's name and introduce himself just as if that person were sitting up in a chair. The chaplain should lean in close so his breath can be felt and his words can be heard. If it is a patient the chaplain has met before and has a relationship with, the chaplain might put his hands on the shoulders or even reach in to kiss the person on the cheek.

During the ritual, the chaplain could reach over to touch the person at particular times. This can happen as the chaplain is speaking of the person or if the person seems to respond to something that has been said. There are times when the whole ritual is done with the chaplain touching the person, if it seems comforting to the patient and/or family. It might be helpful for all of those gathered to place their hands on the patient as they pray.

If it is appropriate, the chaplain can make the sign of the cross on the forehead, if the person held a Christian belief, or simply touch the forehead in blessing. The chaplain can also invite others to do the same. Simply placing a hand on the forehead and saying a blessing of peace is also a way of incorporating sacred touch into the ritual.

Sacred touch may take the form of massage or gentle rubs. Though these may not take place during the ritual, they certainly could. Many patients have expressed a comfort in having their hands or feet rubbed. All of these require permission of the patient as well as training for the chaplain or caregiver.

In the times when the chaplain is called to the bed of someone who has already passed, it is still important that the chaplain touch the body again whether as a sign of blessing or an offer of peace. It is also an important model for those gathered that it is all right to touch this body that held the essence of the loved one.

There are several caveats to be added around touching the deceased. The first concerns disease. As this book was originally being written, Ebola was still spreading in West Africa, and the world was preparing to prevent its spread. The funeral practices of the people of West Africa had been pointed to as a main way this disease was spread, including touching, caressing, and even prostrating oneself on the dead loved one's body. One must follow the advice of the medical official who has pronounced the death of the person. There may be a reason that touching the body is not being allowed. Even if there is no sign of disease, proper hand hygiene is important after touching a body living or dead, and hands should be washed to protect oneself and other loved ones.

The second caveat involves perinatal loss. If a preterm baby has been born and has not survived the birth or died soon afterwards, the skin and bones underneath are very fragile, especially on the head. Great care must be taken in touching this area and should be avoided if possible. Parents are generally encouraged to touch the hands and feet, and in the death ritual the chaplain may also do so, with great care.

As with any of these rituals, the chaplain should be mindful of the expressed needs of the family gathered and of the patient. For instance, in some Buddhist traditions, the belief is that touching a dying person distracts that person from transitioning, and according to that belief, touching may actually keep the soul from passing to the afterlife. This might be especially difficult for paid caregivers when they are attending a patient. In this case, touch is to be minimized as the patient prepares to die.

Additionally, there may be other reasons the person may not want to be touched. Victims of abuse may find any touch or particularly touch by one gender as being intrusive and hurtful. And some patients are simply private. The chaplain will find it helpful to ask permission of the patient or those present as to whether touch is appropriate.

Finally, in the case of a violent death or the sudden death of a child, touching may not be allowed by the law enforcement authorities. It can be a very sad time for parents and other members of the family, and yet it is important that chaplains help family cope with this extra loss.

Bathing

Bathing is considered to be the final act that can be performed by loved ones for the dead. Many cultures have ritualized this final event and prescribe certain plants, herbs, or oils that should be used. In Islam there is great care in the washing of the body, which should be done by Muslims of the same gender, though exceptions are made for the spouse and in the case of children. The body is washed an odd number of times and the final wash is done with water soaked in lotus leaves and camphor if available.[42]

But even the non-ritualistic bathing of the body is a spiritual act that allows the family to grieve the loss and celebrate the life. People tell stories of the scars and markings on the body of their loved one as they bathe the body for the last time. Many times they will kiss or caress each limb in loving response. Such behavior is to be encouraged and celebrated. In her book *Here If You Need Me*, Chaplain Kate Braestrup tells the story of bathing her husband's body after he had been killed in a motorcycle collision. She said, "I will be able to tell myself that I bore our love with my own hands all the way to the last hard place."[43]

It is also important to note that many times hospice patients die either during or shortly after being bathed. It seems as if the act of washing away the final elements of this world gives permission for the person to leave this realm of existence.

Appendix 3 lists a ritual that can be used for family members, nurses, or other caregivers as they bathe a body of a patient after death. The use of water is not necessary in this ritual. Oil or simple touch can also be used.

Clothing and Grooming

Before or even after death, a patient or family member may wish to be dressed in special or comfortable clothing. These clothes might have some special meaning for the patient, might be favorite clothing, or might just be comfortable. In some cultures, the dying are dressed in a particular color or type of clothing. Some cultures believe the person should die in the clothing she will want to wear in the next life. The important thing is that the clothing the patient wears be intentional and of course, if possible, comfortable. This too can be a special symbol for the dying.

Many patients, especially women, have requested that their hair be done, nails be painted, and their make-up be right. Some men want to have their beard/stubble shaved or hair trimmed. Though this may not seem to be important to the loved ones, those simple gestures might help the patient feel "more human" and complete.

Other cultures may find it important that the patient have ceremonial paints or decorations on the patient's face or body. Again the importance of these aspects is based on the culture and beliefs of the patient. It is important to take the patient into account any time a decision is made.

Specific Practices

There are times when a family or patient requests a specific practice or ritual. Sometimes these are tied to a specific religion or culture. It is acceptable for a chaplain to ask, "Close to the time of death, are there certain practices you would like for us to follow?" The family may not know right away, but the chaplain should be open to hearing about these later.

Never assume that a practice from one family or culture will apply broadly to all. Recall from our earlier discussion the young chaplain, who understood from another chaplain that at the time of death Hindus prefer to be on the ground. He helped the care team lower the bed as close to the ground as they could, but when he applied that to the next Hindu patient, he discovered that this was not within their tradition. That chaplain learned an important lesson: never to assume that a belief is practiced across the culture.

Specific Ministers

The use of the term "minister" here refers to any spiritual leader from any religious system or practice. There are times when it becomes very important to have a minister of a specific religion present for a dying patient. Many Catholic (and even former Catholic) patients want a priest there to give last rites, for instance. If a family requests a specific minister or simply a minister from their religion, the chaplain should facilitate this request to the best of his ability and not make this a personal criticism.

It is helpful to cultivate relationships with various religious leaders in the area so the chaplain can call upon them when needed. If it is a new religion for the chaplain or one for which he is not sure how to reach leaders, Internet resources can provide a wealth of information.

The family may have the name of a minister or a place of worship. It is acceptable to ask them for the information, but if they do not know, the chaplain should do his best not to burden them.

There have been times when a chaplain has had ministers tell him that he can do as good a job as they can and should do it. The chaplain can then gently tell the minister that the family has requested a minister from their tradition and ask that if they cannot come, could they recommend someone who could. A chaplain can even go so far as to ask the minister if he would talk to the family over the phone rather than have the chaplain relay the message.

Once a minister has been called, the chaplain should do his best to meet the minister and explain the situation. If it is a minister the family already knows, the chaplain should not feel it is necessary to introduce them, but he should allow the minister to go on in without the chaplain. There have been times when a minister will invite a chaplain to stay and even participate in the ritual. At those times the minister may be giving the message to the patient and family that the chaplain is to be trusted and welcomed into the spiritual care of the person.

Pets

Though pets are not necessarily symbols or rituals, their importance to the dying patient cannot be overlooked. Pets who have been with a patient throughout an illness are also important touchstones for the Spiritual in times of crisis and passing. Generally, these pets are cats or dogs, and some may be protective or standoffish when a chaplain comes in. Other times pets are birds or fish or other animals that have taken a place in the family. One patient commented that the birds outside of her window had become as pets to her, and they seemed to know what was going on. Even in the winter she felt that some had stayed on to keep her company.

Though not all chaplains are animal lovers, it is important as much as possible to allow the pet to be a part of the ministry that is taking place. Whether it means including the pet in the blessing, sharing in the love of the pet by petting it, or simply acknowledging its importance in discussion with the patient, the patient and family would appreciate knowing that the chaplain recognizes that connection to the Spiritual.

A question that might come to mind is what will happen to the pet after the patient dies, especially if the patient lives alone. It may not be a comfortable question to ask the patient, but the chaplain should be ready to discuss it if the topic comes up. Another option is to discuss the topic with a family member beyond the visit with the patient. Sometimes family members do not know what will happen and asking the question may spur a needed discussion. They might need ideas or suggestions. The chaplain should acquaint himself with rescue organizations in the area to offer assistance if requested.

Gratitude

Gratitude, although not one of the tangible symbols and rituals, can be an important touchstone to the Spiritual for patients and families. It is a question that may be raised in the discussion of what patients are happiest about or proudest of in their lives. This gratitude may have been spoken of as family members and patient have spoken to each other.

At times an overarching attitude of gratitude can be inspired and inspiring. Patients may speak of being thankful for each day they have left and how to use that time to celebrate their life. Helping family members to also see this time in terms of gratitude will also connect them to the awareness of the Spiritual. It can also help to alleviate some of the fear, worries, and doubts those gathered may have about the approaching death. Gratitude also gives meaning to the life and experiences.

However, gratitude cannot be forced on a situation. Just as with any of these symbols and rituals, gratitude becomes empty and meaningless if those present do not see its importance. Again the chaplain has to be guided by the family and patient in its use and take clues from the language patterns of those gathered. For some families, the past may be described in pain or hurt, family systems may have broken down, and gratitude may be hard to find.

CHAPTER 4

A Framework for Rituals

The two mothers of this child had very different religious backgrounds. But each time the child was admitted to the hospital I would arrive with a mezuzah, wearing a kippah, and carrying a Jewish prayer book as well as a Bible. The prayer was a combination of Jewish, Catholic, and Pagan spirituality with a bit of Dora the Explorer thrown in. They still remember me as their non-Jewish rabbi.

In order to integrate symbols and rituals, it is critical to put them in the context of the interaction of the chaplain/patient/those gathered. To create a common framework for this discussion, consider the following organizer as a way for the chaplain to use symbols and rituals in the deathbed continuum.

- Acknowledging the Patient and Establishing Rapport
- Assessing the Traditions and Determining Ritual
- Communicating Purpose
- Creating Space
- Connecting Elements
- Sharing Support and Personalizing the Experience
- Blessing/Reflecting
- Closing and Taking Leave

Each of these will be explored in detail and will provide the resources for the chaplain with limited information and limited time to serve the patient at the deathbed in a way that is spiritually meaningful.

Acknowledging the Patient and Establishing Rapport

In order to establish the appropriateness of the use of symbol and ritual at the deathbed, the chaplain must first assess and establish rapport. Acknowledging the dying patient is a critical step and one that is sometimes left out. The dying patient is the central reason for the gathering. It is important that the patient be acknowledged in a way that is receptive and permissive to her need. Rather than starting a ritual, it is important to ask permission and suggest to the patient options for creating a spiritual moment. To some patients the word ritual may not have meaning and for others it may have a negative connotation, so framing this offer in the broadest and most inclusive language possible is important and necessary. In a very real sense the chaplain is invading the space of this loved one and may be a stranger to some gathered, and permission allows for the greatest meaning. The chaplain should never force a ritual on a patient.

Even patients who are apparently unresponsive should be acknowledged and offered the ritual. Though the chaplain may not get a response, the mere act of introducing himself and asking for permission supports the dignity of the patient.

Consider this example. One chaplain had the experience of being asked by the grandmother of a four-year-old boy to pray for the boy (patient) while visiting the two of them in their hospital room. The boy told the chaplain "no," so the chaplain asked if he could pray for the patient's grandmother instead. The patient reluctantly agreed but then cut the chaplain off halfway through with a loud and prayer-terminating "Amen." The prayer was obviously over at that point. That boy showed the importance of asking permission as well as being responsive to the needs or requests of those being visited.

Family and Friends Gathered

There are times when the dying may not know who is gathered around them. It is important to name these people for the dying, especially if they are in a nonresponsive state. Similarly, the chaplain may assure those gathered that the dying person knows they are there. Many times chaplains have been asked this very question, "Do you think she knows I am here?" The best response is to state, "Absolutely," and then encourage those gathered to continue to remind the dying loved one that they are there and how much that person means to them. Also encourage people to tell stories, recall favorite memories, and recite poetry or sing songs the dying person may have enjoyed.

Consider this example. A patient in the hospital at the deathbed seemed to be hanging on beyond what the family expected. She was not dying in the timeframe that they or her care team had anticipated, and this caused the family a great deal of discomfort. The family had done everything they felt they could. The chaplain asked if everyone had been there to say their goodbyes. The family responded that everyone had been there except a favorite granddaughter, who was taking final exams back east. The chaplain suggested they get her on the phone and have her talk to her grandmother and say her goodbye. Though the woman was in an unresponsive state, they held the phone up to her ear as the granddaughter reminded her grandmother of their love for each other and recalled favorite memories. The woman died peacefully the next day. Was the patient waiting for that goodbye? No one knows, but it seemed to bring her peace. It is an important step in the farewell to this life to know that those you love and who love you are present.

Acknowledging the Presence of Others

Establishing rapport may also involve others gathered. A common occurrence and one that can be disconcerting to those gathered is the presence of others, unseen to those present but apparently visible from the perspective of the patient. Many dying patients seem to be visited by people in their life who have died before them. This can be a scary time for the family members and at times for the dying person as well. It is important to acknowledge the fact that it is happening, normalizing it and, when appropriate, inviting the loved ones to stay for the prayers and rituals.

Many ancient peoples and religions speak of their ancestors being present and leading them, especially at the time of death. These ancestors bring protection and wisdom as well as acting as guides for the dying to the next world, life, or realm. These visions can also be quite scary to the family members gathered, especially those who are still in denial that the loved one is dying. Helping these family members acknowledge and welcome passed loved ones or family members may also help to speed their acceptance and healing.

Assessing the Traditions and Determining Ritual

In order for symbols and rituals to be meaningful, the chaplain or the spiritual care provider should assess the patient's tradition and then determine symbols and rituals that might be appropriate. In the preceding section, as chaplains establish rapport with the patient and those gathered, they may gather information about the spiritual tradition beyond the religion listed on the admission sheet. This assessment should be broad and permissive, generally anchored in the form of simple guiding questions.

If permission is granted to proceed with a spiritual ritual, as noted in the preceding section, and the chaplain has a sense of the traditions of the patient, then the chaplain should thoughtfully select symbols and rituals and then proceed.

Remember that receiving permission may be as simple as asking, "Would it be alright if we...?" However, it is important that patient and family be given the chance to agree and participate in the ritual.

Communicating Purpose

As illustrated in the examples included in the next chapter, the chaplain communicates the purpose of the ritual. This is not an elaborate or lengthy discourse. It is a simple acknowledgement of the purpose for what will come next.

Consider these purpose statements: "I would like to lead you (patient and family) through a simple time of reflection and blessing to ease suffering and to bring some peace." Or, "If it is all right with you, I would like to spend a few minutes reading a passage and saying a blessing with you to bring you some peace and comfort." In cases when it is a family member who has summoned the chaplain to the bedside, the chaplain could also ask permission of the patient: "Your spouse asked me to come say a blessing for you as you get close to the end of this journey. I hope that it is all right with you if I do so." If the patient is unresponsive a chaplain can assume permission, but should still look for signs of distress, like furrowed brows or turning the head away from the chaplain.

Creating Space

The space that the patient is in is an important part of ritual. Even in the most confined places such as a hospital room, it is possible to clear space so all may participate. The chaplain must, of course, be respectful of other paid caregivers. An invitation to those present will also give permission for people to leave.

If the television or music is too loud, the chaplain can ask if they can turn it down temporarily. Though some sounds of equipment in a hospital room will never be silenced, there have been times, especially after a death, that the heart monitor will continue to go off. Asking a nurse to be present to stop such noises is an appropriate request.

Lighting should also be considered. Lights can be dimmed and blinds opened or closed to provide a more spiritual atmosphere.

Finally, at the beginning of the ritual, the chaplain can use an element of air either through a chime, a singing bowl, or simply asking people to take a breath to clear the space and connect to the Spiritual.

Connecting Elements

This is the time for the use of symbols and perhaps the ritual itself. The connecting elements include the symbols, perhaps the readings, or

other relational and connecting elements that are accessible spiritually
to the patient. In addition to the elemental symbols explored in chapter
3, others will be explored in the next chapter. Again, examples of how
to use these connecting elements will be provided.

Sharing Support and Personalizing the Experience

On the deathbed continuum, the patient and those gathered are often
expecting some opportunity to participate and are often hopeful that
the chaplain has a personal connection to the situation. As the chaplain
uses symbols and rituals, there is an opportunity for others to share
words, stories, and memories.

An important part of the bedside ritual will be the telling of stories
and recalling of memories. A good way to start any spiritual care visit,
from wedding planning to funeral planning, is to say, "Tell me about
yourselves/your loved one." It opens a whole new view of the relationship and allows the chaplain to see immediately what is important, as
that is what people remember and will share with the chaplain.

In one instance, when a chaplain was called to the emergency room
of a woman who had died unexpectedly, her children and grandchildren
present told stories of her being a quilter but noted that she had not
been able to quilt for several years because of her eyesight. The patient
also loved to dance but had not done that since their father had died
several years ago. So in the blessing the chaplain was able to send her
off to a place where she could dance once again with her husband and
create a new quilt of love to surround her children and grandchildren
so they would always know she was there.

Another gentleman was a greeter at a local store and had died on
the job. When the chaplain met his son and daughter in the emergency room, they told the chaplain how much he loved doing that
job. Tears came to the chaplain's eyes as he remembered seeing the
patient in his role at the store. The blessing that followed included
sending him off to a place where he might continue greeting new-
comers from this life.

Stories and memories are the connections that loved ones will need to hold on to and will make the bedside ritual even more important. These too are symbols that can connect the patient, family, and chaplain to the spiritual story that makes up the ritual. Storytelling and recalling memories will help the healing process as well as helping the chaplain to make important connections with the patient and family.

Blessing/Reflecting

A simple blessing or reflection may close a ritual. These blessings should be broad, inclusive, and accessible. It is critical to not impose a particular religious connotation on the blessing.

The word "blessing" has been used many times throughout this study. Sometimes that is a misunderstood word. In the sense it is used here, it could be a form of a prayer that may or may not have any God-language at all. The blessing should depend on the needs and beliefs of those present. A blessing in this context is the reality that there is a spiritual occasion here. A life is passing out of this realm of existence and, whether the beliefs of the patient and those present include an afterlife, rebirth, or reincarnation, or an assumption that the end of life means the end of existence, the loved one will continue on through the memories and love of those present. A blessing in a real sense seeks to celebrate that reality.

So in the blessing the chaplain will seek to recapture the things that have been talked about up until that time. The chaplain might incorporate stories and images, recall special people and events, and invite the spiritual reality and sacredness of the occasion to manifest in this present time. If there are particular prayers to be said, this is the time to incorporate them, including any corporate prayers, for instance, "The Lord's Prayer" for Christians. The chaplain might invite others to add their own blessings along with his. The chaplain might ask the family to touch the patient as they do the blessing. Even with written or prescribed prayers, the blessing could be a highly personal time for those present.

The blessing may take the form of prayer. Many times if the patient or family has requested a chaplain to visit the deathbed, they want prayers to be said. These prayers can either be spontaneous or written or a combination of both. Knowing the spiritual background of the patient, as well as the family and friends gathered, is foundational to being able to provide the best and most healing experience for all of those present. There are times when the needs of the patient or even some of those present are going to be at odds with each other. This is especially true when the family members are of various beliefs or backgrounds.

At times there will be family members opposed to any kind of prayer, as well as those who specifically believe that calling on the name of a sacred entity, for instance, Jesus or Allah, is vitally important. Of course, if the patient is alert, it is best to ask the patient what she would want at this time. If the patient is not able to answer, asking those closest to the patient what they believe the patient would want is also appropriate.

Asking permission from family members opposed to specific religious practices also is helpful. Giving them permission not to be present during that time and offering them their own time of blessing or celebration is sometimes helpful. It is sometimes helpful to frame it by saying this would be helpful to the patient or to the family members requesting the religious time.

In this case if a religious practice is allowed, using the broadest and most inclusive spiritual language will be very important to this family. Celebrating the life and recalling the special blessings the patient gave to this family will be an important way to include the widest number of family members present. In this way the chaplain will gain the trust of each person present.

There might also come a time when a chaplain will be forced to choose a path. In that case the chaplain may find it necessary to follow the wishes of either the patient or the main decision maker of the family. It is important to maintain focus and provide guidance. Chaplains are there to provide the spiritual support, and it is important to that they not lose site of this reality.

There may also be a reason that a chaplain cannot be at the bedside. Perhaps the chaplain is ministering to people who have been banned from the room. Perhaps the main caregiver has decided not to allow spiritual support there. Perhaps due to cultural concerns, that chaplain is not allowed in, as in the case of a male chaplain and a female Hindu patient. There might be a literal space between the chaplain and family he is supporting and the patient, for instance, if the patient is in another part of the country or even world. Perhaps the patient is incarcerated or in isolation.

At these times it is important to offer the blessing in an alternate space. It might be in the chaplain's office or a chapel, outside in a prayer garden, or even in the home of the patient or family member. It is easy to remember that spiritual care is given to the person present with you and that that person is connected to the patient. It might be beneficial to have a picture or linking object at hand. Continue the ritual as planned, just as if the patient were present.

One time a chaplain was asked by the mother of a patient to pray for urine output from her young son, who was in a coma. The doctors had told this mother that it was the indication they needed to see if the internal organs were still functioning. The chaplain suggested praying at the bedside, but the mother asked the chaplain to do it elsewhere, as she did not want her son to be disturbed. She also did not want to leave the boy's side. The chaplain gathered a couple of chaplain residents and went to the chapel. They had a prayer circle there for urine output. The mother believed that prayers would be heard wherever they were said. (The boy did eventually recover fully.)

Sometimes families ask for specific things. The difficult part is if they ask and expect a miracle healing. Many times a chaplain will have a discussion about what healing might look like. That healing might still end with the patient's death, but some spiritual and relationship healing could take place for patient and family.

There is also a time to check for what the family understands from the physicians and healthcare providers. If the chaplain senses they do not understand the severity of the disease progression, then it is important to reengage the healthcare team, and perhaps the chaplain can offer to be there as the situation is explained again. This especially happens if a family member arrives later on the scene. Though this check for understanding might come after the blessing time, the chaplain should still be aware of it and activate other members of the care team as well.

Some families feel that if the chaplain has hesitation about praying for the miracle, then he is causing more harm than good. At that time, it is important to offer to have someone else to pray for them. Perhaps they have a minister in mind whom the chaplain can call. Perhaps there is another chaplain who, given the chance, would be happy to oblige the family's wishes.

Closing and Taking Leave

Finally, the chaplain closes the ritual and takes leave. Prolonged ritual may interfere with end-of-life care, and closing is a way to signal to the patient and family that the chaplain must take leave. The symbols used during the ritual may remain.

The chaplain should always close the ritual time with some words that help the family and patient know that it is complete. If it is a religious time, then ending "In the name of God" will signify this completion. One way to say this is, "In the many names of God we pray," which recognizes the abundance of spiritualties that might be present.

If this has been a Christian time of ritual and blessing, adding "in the precious name of Jesus" is a way of ending the time. If a time of Christian anointing will take place, the chaplain can anoint thus: "In the name of the Father, and of the Son, and of the Holy Spirit."

If the ritual and time of blessing has been a nonreligious event or if there are various faith traditions present, the chaplain might close the ritual with "I grant you Peace, and Light, and Love" or similar words.

Each religious tradition might have different ways of closing a ritual. If the chaplain is using a prayer from a tradition that is different from one he is used to, closing with this prayer is also completely appropriate and helpful to those present. If a chime or singing bowl has been used, this also can signify the end of the ritual and in turn can help clear the space.

In the next chapter we will see how some of the symbols and rituals discussed thus far can be used in the continuum of care at the deathbed and beyond. These symbols and this format will be used in rituals for patients in various scenarios and contexts as well as in rituals for the family beyond death and throughout the grief process.

CHAPTER 5

Suggested Rituals to Be
Used at the Deathbed and Afterwards

*The patient was non-responsive and near death. Gathered were
many family members with belief systems that ranged from Jewish
to Born Again Christian to Neo-Pagan to Atheist. But they were
gathered for a sacred time to say goodbye to the patient. Using
music, a singing bowl, readings, sacred elements from seashore and
art as well as individual times of speaking, the chaplain led the
family through a Spiritual experience where each felt welcomed
and supported, and the patient left this realm knowing she was
loved and blessed.*

This study has explored symbols and rituals that cross traditions
and those that are personally identified and selected by the patient
and those gathered at the deathbed. In order to illustrate the practical
implication of this discourse, the chaplain might rely on and adapt the
examples provided. What follows are several rituals that have been used
with patients in different places and at various times. These rituals were
developed from multiple visits with various patients.

The study of the different rituals included in this chapter were
generally aligned with the framework presented in the previous chapter. This flow affords the chaplain an adaptable structure when meeting

patients and their families and then attending to their spiritual needs through symbol and ritual. Each of these was explained in detail in Chapter 4 and will be illustrated in the following examples of rituals at the deathbed. As a reminder, this framework is:

- Acknowledging the Patient and Establishing Rapport
- Assessing the Traditions and Determining Ritual
- Communicating Purpose
- Creating Space
- Connecting Elements
- Sharing Support and Personalizing the Experience
- Blessing/Reflecting
- Closing and Taking Leave

In order to avoid redundancy in these examples only the components that are unique to the context are included. The framework presented in Chapter 4 is intended to guide the process, whereas the examples provided in this chapter are intended to illustrate the content of certain components within specific contexts noted below. These rituals are organized around several variations of the deathbed continuum. Each of the variations creates the need for the chaplain to adapt certain components of the specified framework. Consider consciousness, those gathered, and the point on the deathbed continuum to guide determination of ritual and symbol.

Primarily the chaplain must acknowledge the state of consciousness of the patient, responsive or nonresponsive. The selection of the ritual will vary based on this information. Oftentimes the rituals for the nonresponsive patient have as the primary purpose to bring comfort to those gathered. Next, the chaplain must assess who is present. Rituals will vary according to who is gathered if there are any persons gathered at all. Some patients are surrounded by many people while others, by choice or circumstance, die alone. And finally, these rituals are intended to provide examples from all points of the deathbed continuum—before death, at the time of death, after death. From the active death of the patient to the extended periods of grief for those gathered, now those surviving, the chaplain is equipped with symbols and rituals that may provide common structures for uncommon clients.

Ritual at the Deathbed—
Patient Nonresponsive and Family Gathered

Acknowledging the
Patient and Establishing Rapport

When a chaplain is called in to do a ritual for a nonresponsive patient, it is many times an opportunity for the family to say goodbye and begin the grief and healing processes. The chaplain should take time to acknowledge the patient, even though she is unresponsive, and the chaplain should introduce himself. The chaplain should also get to know those gathered, assessing their relationships to the patient and their expectations for this time.

Assessing the
Traditions and Determining Ritual

Part of getting to know those who are gathered might include asking about their religious traditions. Many times families will have various traditions. If possible the chaplain should try to incorporate these traditions. At this time the chaplain may look for symbols and signs of ritual around the room.

Communicating Purpose

There may be various reasons for this gathering. Hopefully the family is gathered to say goodbye and to honor the patient. There could also be unresolved differences between family members and maybe even with the patient. If the chaplain is simply aware of these issues, he can be ready to redirect or suggest dealing with these outside of the patient's room. At this point the chaplain may clarify that this ritual is specifically to acknowledge the patient and the death.

Creating Space

The chaplain could use a singing bowl or chime to clear the space before the ritual. This is a way of using the element of air to begin this ritual. The chaplain could then use a reading. Suggestions could be the poet Mary Oliver's "In Blackwater Woods," Mark Nepo's "Joel at 94," or the "23rd Psalm" if people gathered agree it would be appropriate. Each of these is listed in Appendix 1. If the chaplain notices a music player in the room, he might ask if there is special music they would like to play for the patient.

The chaplain should also notice if there are pictures of the patient and family, some artwork, or other special items, including religious artifacts. If it is appropriate, a candle can be lit as an additional way of using the element of fire.

Sharing Support and Personalizing the Experience

The chaplain invites the family around the bed in a circle. The chaplain leans down and explains to the patient who is there and why they are gathered. The chaplain expresses to the patient that they all know her time is near and wish to say their goodbyes together. The chaplain also asks the patient if she is seeing loved ones from the other side, asks if they are calling to her, and notes that, if so, these loved ones are welcomed into the circle as well. The chaplain should watch for patient reactions.

Though the patient does not seem responsive, the chaplain should tell the patient about the singing bowl or chime that will be used. After ringing the bowl, if the patient shows no signs of discomfort, the chaplain rings it a second time, and as it rings he invites everyone to take in a deep breath, release any tension they might have, and breathe in the love that this patient had for each of them. The chaplain reminds them to continue this deep breathing throughout their time together. The chaplain should follow this with the reading that has been selected.

Sharing Support and Personalizing the Experience

Storytelling and reminiscing are ways to share support and personalize the experience. So the chaplain asks, "Tell me your favorite things about your loved one and memories of your life with her." And for several minutes allow the family to recount stories and memories, painting the picture of the person whom they knew. They may use the personal symbols found in the space to help tell their stories. The chaplain should listen to the stories, ask leading questions, and respond appropriately. As the stories slow down, the chaplain might ask about a song they want to play for the patient. If they have one, allow the family to talk about why it is an important memory. After they play the song, then allow the music to transition into a quiet, meditative time.

Blessing/Reflecting

At this point the chaplain should lead the group in a time of reflection, recalling many of the stories they have shared and noting how these were important facets that make up the loved one and their memory of her. Use these memories to remind the loved ones gathered that each time they participate in similar experiences going forward—whether viewing or creating art pieces, visiting places, or doing activities that were spoken of—loved ones can see these as ways to connect back to the memories and thus to the patient. The chaplain can continue the reflection, reminding the patient that her work here is finished, and that she is free to leave this realm when she is ready. It is important to state that her family will be okay and that they are united in their love of her and her love of them.

Closing and Taking Leave

The chaplain can end the time with an appropriate reading, prayer, or blessing such as a prayer from one of the traditions gathered, a favorite poem, or even reading again the piece that was read earlier. There are many suggestions in Appendix 1. The chaplain should take care to read the piece in a quiet, peaceful tone, not being afraid to pause often or even repeat phrases to allow the words to sink in.

The chaplain might then allow a time for the family to offer their own prayers or pieces of wisdom. If no one wishes to speak, then the chaplain should be ready to close off the time with a final few words. Then the chaplain can ring the singing bowl again and allow this to signal the end of their time together.

The chaplain should take his leave of the patient as well as the family. As always, the chaplain should ask if there is anything else he can do for the family. If this is to be an ongoing support, the chaplain should make sure the family knows how to get in touch with him.

It is also important for the chaplain to take leave of the patient. Even though the patient is unresponsive, taking this extra step shows respect to the patient and serves as a good example to the family.

Ritual at the Deathbed— Conscious Patient Gathered with Family

Acknowledging the Patient and Establishing Rapport

If the chaplain has not met this patient before, and the patient feels like talking, do some exploring around her beliefs, fears, and hopes. Three questions that are helpful are:

- In your life, what are you happiest or proudest of?
- Is there anything you wish you could have changed in your life?
- Do you have any fears or concerns?

The answers to these three questions help frame the ritual. It is also good to ask the patient and family present about favorite pastimes, hobbies, or memories. Using these informs the ritual and may allow for the chaplain to determine linking symbols.

Assessing the Traditions and Determining Ritual

If the chaplain has learned something of the patient or family's religious views or roles, those may be incorporated into the ritual—perhaps in the choice of phrasing—but this must be within the comfort zone of the chaplain. This may not be a time to ask for a full description of the death rituals of a particular faith, but the chaplain can ask if there are any rituals that they would like to have at this time.

Communicating Purpose

The purpose of this gathering in part depends on the state of the patient. If the patient is doing well at this point, this may be a time of prayer for healing in the broader view. If the patient is getting close to death, the family may be gathered to say their goodbyes as the above example showed. Added to this, the chaplain may not know until he is at the deathbed with the family. This purpose should be apparent with a few well placed questions about patient or family expectations. "Why are we gathered today?" or "What can I do for you today?"

Creating Space

The chaplain will find it important to pause and create a spiritual space for those present. If it is appropriate, ask those gathered to join hands or invite them to move closer and touch the patient. Be sure to phrase it as a suggestion, for instance, "If it is all right, I would like to invite everyone to..."

Invite everyone to take a deep breath and exhale slowly. Do this at least three times inviting them to breath in light and peace and exhale their anxiety and worry. This elemental connection calms the fears and often the complex decision-making that those gathered have been challenged with. If a bowl, chime, or bell is available, ring this as an ending to this clearing time. If not, simply invite people to return to the present state.

Connecting Elements

If the chaplain knows the patient, he may already know of a reading, poem, or piece of literature that is important to them. If he does not know the patient, ask now for a suggestion or ask if she would like you to choose one for her. If it is appropriate, the 23rd Psalm is a well-known and accepted reading. There are variations that make the psalm, a traditional Judeo-Christian scripture, less specifically religious. See Appendix 1 for examples. "Desiderata" is another reading that helps to engage the Spirit. The chaplain might be able to choose a favorite reading from the spiritual background of the person. "When Death Comes" by Mary Oliver is also an appropriate reading to have available for these times. These as well as other suggestions are also listed in Appendix 1.

Sharing Support and Personalizing the Experience

Assuming others are present with the patient, this is a time when the chaplain might speak to the patient about the strength and message he hears in this reading. This is also the time to speak to the fears, worries, happy memories, and favorite pastimes that the chaplain might have gathered. If appropriate, speak about family members who are precious and perhaps those who are far away.

This is also the time to invite others to speak to each other, perhaps asking family members to share with the patient a special memory or a happy time. Asking them to share what they learned from the patient and how the patient will continue to live through them is another important support to the patient as well as the family members.

Finally, this is also a time to allow the patient a chance to say anything she would like to her family that is gathered. She may not have much energy to speak, but if she wants to, it will be an important connection. These words can be difficult in the moment, so if there is time, the chaplain might collect some of the patient's thoughts beforehand and either provide prompting or ask permission to share these thoughts for this part of the ritual.

Blessing/Reflecting

This is a time to offer and invite. A chaplain can play a pivotal role in making this time a spiritual experience. Using symbols such as water, oil, or just touch, the chaplain should ask permission to touch the patient (most likely on the forehead) and say some words of blessing. Introduction of these elemental symbols is often familiar and comforting to many, but as in all parts of ritual, the chaplain gently guides the process through permission seeking and suggestion. The words could be specific to the patient's religious background. However, a nonreligious blessing is also helpful. An example could be:

May you be free of fear, and know that you are cared for;

May you be free of concern, and rest in peacefulness;

May your body and mind be free of pain, and may your spirit find comfort.

Know you are a precious child and are loved beyond all telling.

The chaplain can then invite the others gathered who are comfortable in doing so to also touch the patient and express their love or blessing to her in their own words or from their own faith tradition.

Closing and Taking Leave

The blessing time may be quite a powerful and emotional experience for the patient and those gathered. It will be helpful for the chaplain to be ready to close the time so those gathered have a vessel to hold the experience. There are various prayers or blessings that can bring this time to a close. A chaplain can certainly use his own words. Some chaplains prefer a written blessing that can be read. "Entering Death" by John O'Donohue is one such appropriate reading.

A chaplain should thank the patient and the family gathered for their time and ask if there is anything else that he can offer. Even if death is near, it is important to remind the patient of the chaplain's continued support, thoughts, and prayers.

Ritual for Near Death—Patient Is Alone

Perhaps the most difficult time to be with a patient for the chaplain is when the patient is alone and coming in and out of consciousness. There is a feeling that no one wants to die alone, and in fact there is an established program that many hospices and hospitals use called *No One Dies Alone* that provides volunteers to sit with patients who are close to death and either have no one sitting with them or whose family simply cannot be there. Sometimes dying alone is a matter of choice and at other times it is a matter of complex and hurtful circumstance.

But the reality is that many patients die when loved ones or caregivers have simply slipped out of the room for a few minutes. Chaplains have heard that story often and many times have personal stories around that reality. A chaplain can use this as an opportunity to alleviate the concern that dying alone is a horrible fate. For some, dying without anyone in attendance is a way to relieve their loved ones of any grief. Others perhaps see death as the most personal of moments and enter death alone or unaided.

That being said, there is a ritual for that that circumstance when the patient is alone and the chaplain steps in to visit for a while. The chaplain's role may simply be for comfort and presence. Even so, the chaplain can follow a simple plan to make this a time of spiritual connection.

Acknowledging the Patient and Establishing Rapport

Regardless of whether the patient seems to be cognizant of her surroundings or not, the chaplain should begin by acknowledging the patient, introducing himself, and explaining his role.

Assessing the Traditions and Determining Ritual

When the chaplain does not know the patient, the chaplain should scan the room for personal symbols. Take note of anything in the room that can help frame this sacred time. Flowers indicate this patient has someone who loves her. A stuffed animal or blanket are signs of comfort and may have a story that is locked away from the chaplain, and yet these objects can be used as anchor points. Are there religious artifacts that may give an indication of the patient's religious leanings? A Bible, a rosary, a prayer rug, a *kippah* (yarmulke), a picture of a yogi, or a statue of the Buddha are all signs of various religions. These symbols could also include jewelry that perhaps the patient is wearing. A cross, a star of David, or an Om can help guide the chaplain in this time. Are there books that could show the patient's interest? A spy novel or a dog magazine may not indicate much, but it is a start in helping to engage the patient's interests. Alternatively, the music on the radio or station on the television may or may not be indicative of the patient (it may have just been what was on), but a chaplain can still use this.

Communicating Purpose

The chaplain should engage the patient and explain why he is there. If the chaplain has had a relationship with the patient, that will be relatively easy. If the patient is new to the chaplain, perhaps the chaplain will give a brief explanation of his role and what he hopes to accomplish with this visit.

Creating Space

Once some quick information has been gathered, the chaplain can now begin to engage the patient. The chaplain should speak as if the patient can respond. Encourage the patient to think of those people who gave her flowers, feel the comfort of the stuffed animal, or offer to read an excerpt from the book or magazine that is there. This creates a spiritual tone to a visit by letting the patient know she matters.

Connecting Elements

The chaplain should refer back to the elements that he noticed and any information he collected from the patient. If the chaplain knows anything about the loved ones of the patient, these are also important connections for him to make at this point.

Sharing Support and Personalizing the Experience

The chaplain could now offer a reading/prayer for the patient. If the patient has a religious preference, the chaplain can use a prayer from her tradition. Readings of psalms, especially 23, 91, and 121, can also comfort many patients, particularly if they have a Judeo-Christian background. Versions can be found in Appendix 1. These can also be adjusted to omit or adapt the God language, focusing instead on the peace or comfort they speak. If the patient has no religious affiliation the chaplain could find a poem or prayer that would have some significance to the patient. One suggestion is to ask the patient if there is a reading she would like to have read. If there is no suggestion, then the chaplain might ask if the patient would like him to choose one. For example, the "Native American Prayer" listed in Appendix 1 is generally accessible and comfortable for many.

Blessing/Reflecting

Perhaps the chaplain has gained enough information to be able to offer a blessing in a religious tradition that is evident from the items in the room. But even if that has not been established, the chaplain can certainly offer a broad blessing of comfort and peace to the patient. The chaplain could use symbols such as oil or water or simply touch (with explanation to/permission of the patient) and say a simple blessing. The chaplain might use the words of blessing from the previous ritual example above.

Closing and Taking Leave

Because the patient is alone, it is important that the chaplain check with the patient to determine if she is all right to be left alone. The chaplain should be prepared to stay longer if needed or access other support services such as volunteers.

A Ritual for the Point of Death with Family Gathered

There are times when the chaplain is present for the very sacred moment when the patient's life ends. At these times it is very important for the chaplain (or any staff) to be ready for a variety of experiences. These times often bring up deep and significant emotions, including extreme grief.

Although the chaplain is there to provide support to the family, he should also be prepared to understand the physical death process, that is, to become acquainted with what happens to the physical body at death. While most hospices have information they share with families to help explain the dying process, it is also critical for the chaplain to know what to expect. It will not help if the chaplain is caught off guard, and the family senses that at this difficult time. A chaplain not prepared for the experience of the death may create a sense of fear; the chaplain's unprepared reaction may be translated as something more significant by those gathered. In other words, those gathered may rely on the chaplain to assure them by normalizing the dying process. A brief explanation of this process can be found in the book *A Clergy Guide to End-of-Life Issues* by Martha Jacobs.[44]

Acknowledging the Patient and Establishing Rapport

The chaplain needs to be prepared that anything can happen with family members once the patient has passed. Even family members who have been expecting this death for months can have difficult reactions. The opposite is also true; family members who are expected to have negative reactions can be quiet and reserved when the death takes place.

With family members who are having a difficult time with the death, the chaplain's role is to create the safe space for them in that experience. Keep them and others gathered as safely as possible. Sometimes this initial emotional reaction may become physical. If necessary, the chaplain should get everyone out of the room and take with him anything that the family member might use to cause more harm. These are rare experiences, but it is good to be prepared and always aware. Generally, the chaplain needs to allow the family members to mourn. After a period of time, taking cues from those gathered, the chaplain can begin a parting ritual.

Assessing the Traditions and Determining Ritual

The deathbed ritual involves both the time during the death and that time immediately after. This is also the time when it is important to know the patient's and family's belief about the body after death. In certain Buddhist beliefs, the body should not be moved or even touched, as this might confuse the soul and delay its departing. As mentioned before, some Hindus prefer to have the body on the ground touching the earth. If the discussion has not been had with the family about what they would like or not like to happen, the chaplain should ask simply, "Is there anything extra you need us to do for your loved one at this time?"

Communicating Purpose

This is simply a time for the chaplain to pause and assure the family he is there for their support and wishes to help their loved one through this transition out of this life.

Creating Space

A prayer at the point of death or a parting reading may serve as an appropriate component. Many traditions have prayers at the point of death that can be used and adjusted. Some of these are listed in Appendix 1. Psalm 23 is again appropriate to use at this time. A simple recitation from *Hamlet* made by Horatio at Hamlet's death may be appropriate.

Now cracks a noble heart. Good night sweet [prince]:
And flights of angels sing thee to thy rest![45]

The word "prince" can be changed to the person's name.

"Desiderata," "Funeral Blues" by W. H. Auden, "On the Death of the Beloved," by John O'Donohue, and "Wild Geese" by Mary Oliver are also appropriate nonreligious readings that can be used and are listed in Appendix 1. It is helpful for the chaplain to already have something in mind and ready to use. This is also a time when other favorite readings might be used to recall the spiritual time that is present.

Sharing Support and Personalizing the Experience

Saying goodbye in its simplest form is a critical part of this ritual. It is also important that the family members present be allowed to say their goodbyes. It can mean simply offering those present to say or do something to give them a sense of closure. Some family members might want to say what the patient meant to them and thank the dying loved one. Some family members may want to kiss their loved one. And some may want to simply stand quietly. All of these reactions are to be expected and accepted. The chaplain needs to realize that this might also be a time when family members who chose to embrace the patient may break down and weep and cling. Again, the chaplain needs to be prepared for the continuum of reactions and provide support.

Connecting Elements

This piece is out of sequence, as it presents a final ritual as a connecting element for the family. An important service might be to offer the family a chance to bathe the body. The chaplain will need coordinate this with the nurse. Some families will decline this service, and it is left to the nurse or aide. But if the family would like to do this, the chaplain can help by providing a ritual around this sacred time. Included in Appendix 3 is a ritual that the palliative care team at a hospital included in this study offers to family members. As mentioned in the introduction, this ritual can be done during bathing or simply performed while the family member or staff person touches or anoints with oil the various parts of the body.

The chaplain does not have to be present for this part of the ritual and in fact may excuse himself to give the family and patient privacy if a full bath is given. However, the chaplain should assess the situation and take direction from the family.

Blessing/Reflecting

After the bathing and the blessing of the body or prior to taking leave of the family and patient, the chaplain could offer a blessing to send off the spiritual presence of the patient. This blessing can be done by repeating all or part of one of the blessings or readings used previously in the ritual, or using a blessing that the chaplain creates, for example:

> [NAME], your journey on this planet has ended
> and death has taken you from our presence.
> May you go now to that place where you will feel no more pain
> and you will be at peace always.
> Know you will always live in our hearts
> and our love for you will never end.

Closing and Taking Leave

As always, it is important for the chaplain to take leave of both the patient and the family. It may seem unusual to take leave of the dead patient, but it shows the family a respect for their loved one. This taking leave can be done simply, by touching the hand of the patient and smiling, or simply wishing the patient peace. Before leaving, the chaplain should ask the family if there is anything else they need.

Extending Support Along the Deathbed Continuum to the After-Death Experiences

After the death, the chaplain may be invited to lead a funeral or memorial service. Leveraging the rituals and symbols described above will provide continuity and connections for those gathered. Similarly, bereavement and grief work is considered in this study as the last component of the deathbed continuum. The following rituals have been used by chaplains and are broad representations, easily adapted by individual chaplains.

Funeral/Memorial Service—Traditional Style

Many families will access their own spiritual leaders to lead funerals and memorial services; however, some families will ask the chaplain who has been with the family throughout the dying process to continue to support them at this time.

It is important to note here that the rituals offered here are frameworks for services. When possible, these services should be developed with the input of the family and perhaps even the patient before death. Memorial services and funerals are for the living, but if the patient has something she would like to have included this becomes an important part of the service.

It is also important to ask the family if there are particular religious or cultural symbols or rituals they would like to have included in the service. Many cultures have specific rituals that should be included. If at all possible, include these or find someone who can act as an intermediary for those parts. A particular prayer in a different language, holy water sprinkled on the casket, or the body being buried facing a particular direction are all important details not to be left out. Some cultures have a belief regarding what colors should be worn by the mourners as well as the officiant of the service.

Beyond religious considerations are traditions that a family might have, such as drinking a toast at the graveside, a particular dance, or some other tradition, so it is important to get input from the family.

Many organizations, including Masons and military, also have traditions that might be important to include. As difficult as it might be for the family, sitting down with the patient to discuss the service beforehand will help discover the little details that are important to them so those things may be included.

Opening Song—Many services begin with a song as people gather. This song could be one that was important to the deceased or simply one picked out by those planning the service. There is a list of possible songs in Appendix 2. If the music is recorded it is important for the chaplain to make sure the sound system is working ahead of time. If the memorial service is taking place in a funeral home, work with the funeral director. If the family is doing the service elsewhere or even outside, the chaplain should take responsibility for double-checking that the system is working.

Greeting—The chaplain should open the service with words of gathering such as:

> "We gather here today to give thanks for the life of _____, who shared her life with us and died on _____, at an age of __ years. It is in her memory that we gather and for her life that we are thankful."

If the obituary is to be read, this is a good place to do so. Even if the entire obituary is not read, it can often help frame some opening remarks.

Invocation—The chaplain will give an invocation at this point. If there is a religious tradition to be followed, the chaplain should use a prayer from that tradition. Other suggestions for invocations are listed in Appendix 1.

Readings—The chaplain could read or have other people read one or several readings at this point. One or two readings should be used, and they should give hope to those gathered.

A suggestion is that close family members should not be asked to read, unless they wish to do so. These readings could be special readings that the family or patient requested or held dear. Many of the readings listed in the Appendix 1 will also work at this time.

Song—see above under "Opening Song" (optional here)

Eulogy—This is a time when a close friend or family member tells a few stories about the life of the deceased that people will identify with. The hope is that they would keep out any personal issues that might cause pain or hurt, but tell a story of how the deceased dealt with the illness that took away life. This eulogy should be scripted so the chaplain or someone else could read it if necessary. And it should end with a commendation of the loved one—"We will miss you, _____, but we know you are off on your next adventure and will always be with us..."

Open Sharing—Some families find it is important to allow an opportunity for anyone who wishes to speak. This can be problematic for a couple of reasons. The first is the obvious one that someone might decide to speak too long or even inappropriately. The second problem is actually more common in that no one steps up to speak. If a family member is insisting on an open sharing time, the chaplain may suggest that that person and perhaps another be identified to start the sharing.

Particular Cultural/Religious Rituals—If the family has requested something special to be done, be sure to include it here or elsewhere in the service.

Song—see above under "Opening Song" (optional here)

Committal—Wording can be adjusted but closing the service with a committal signals to the assembly that the service is concluding. Suggested wording could be:

> "So it is that we gather to commemorate the passing of one who was with us and is no more. We keep in our minds and hearts those memories and that love we knew because _____ shared her life with us; and we commit her body to the ground and her spirit into the keeping of the Eternal Peace."

Closing Invocation—Use a prayer selected by the family, one within the deceased's faith parameters, or one chosen from Appendix 1.

Closing Song—see above.

Memorial Service—Nontraditional Style

Perhaps the most important part of a nontraditional service that the chaplain must attend to is where the service takes place and who is invited. One service was done for an artist who loved the sea and thus was done at the end of a pier. Other sites have included forests, seashores, pubs, and places of business. It is still important that the ritual contain some elements that help participants and perhaps passersby know that someone's life is being remembered.

Music—If music is available (live or recorded), it is often an effective way to begin and end a service.

Introduction—The chaplain should tell part of the person's life. Include in this introduction why the loved ones have selected this unusual space for this memorial.

Obituary or Story of the Person's Death and Life—Though this part is not always necessary, it is a good grounding tool to remind those gathered why they are there. Many loved ones are now writing obituaries that tell more than just the facts, so draw on this information. Some patients may have written their own obituaries as pieces of legacy writing. These should be used and celebrated. A memorial service is an appropriate time to do so.

Eulogy—This might be done by the chaplain or by a friend or family member. It should be by someone who knew the person and has a connection to the life being celebrated.

Personal Sharing—In a nontraditional setting people might be encouraged to speak about their relationship with the deceased.

Closing—This could be a poem or reading important to the person, a song, or a prayer, if appropriate.

Music—One option that has been used in several memorial services is to have "Taps" played, especially if the deceased had a military background. There are many other options that can be used to end this ritual time. Refer to the list in Appendix 2 for other suggestions or ask family members/friends for input.

Final Ritual—If the deceased was cremated and the ashes are to be spread, this would be a time to invite the family to come forth and do so. Alternatively, people might drop a flower into the water, light a candle, or even drink a toast to the departed. Some families use this time to share the departed one's collections with those gathered. As an example, one person had a large collection of shot glasses. The family lined these up on the railing during her service and at the end of the service participants were invited to take a shot glass and use it in some way to keep her memory alive.

Graveside Service and Rituals

Many times there will not be a need for both a service inside and a service at the cemetery or place of internment. However, there might be a slightly different tone to the two actions. What follows is a graveside service that could function as an independent service or as part of the full service.

Opening and Welcome—Gather the family members close. Welcome those and express the reason they are gathered.

Blessing of the Time and Space—Make this a spiritual time by invoking the life that is around and the life that is past. If the deceased or family have a particular religious background, use a blessing from that tradition.

Reading—Share a reading that is important to the deceased or chose one that is appropriate. One of the variations of Psalm 23 could be used at this time. There are many other suggestions in Appendix 1.

Reflection—Share a brief reflection on the reading and incorporate the life of the deceased. If a eulogy has not been done elsewhere, it can be done at this time.

Open Sharing—Those gathered might wish to offer their own thoughts, prayers, or special memories.

Closing Reading—"The Serenity Prayer" is a good concluding prayer to this ritual. There are many other options that can be used.

Farewell Ritual—If ashes are to be spread as part of this service, this would be the time to spread them. If it is a traditional burial of a coffin, this is the time—in the past, and in some traditions still—when the body is lowered into earth. Traditionally the family stepped forward to throw some dirt onto the casket. This acts as a final farewell and makes the death a reality. A way to incorporate this ritual without lowering the body is simply inviting the family forward to place a flower, a pebble, or some other item onto the coffin, tombstone, or gravesite.

Commendation/Benediction—These words or similar ones can be used to close this service:

> We commend our loved one _____ to the earth.
> Though her life with us is over, she will always live in our hearts.
> May we hear her voice in the wind and the singing of birds
> and feel the warmth of her love in the sun on our face.
> Let us go forth from this place in peace to continue to live the life
> that _____ would have wanted us to, knowing that her journey
> on this earth is over, and she truly rests in peace.

Private Rituals

There are times when a loved one cannot make a funeral or memorial service. Perhaps the trip across the distance makes it impossible. There are times when the loved one cannot travel due to finances, health, or timing.

Perhaps it is a trip across time that makes it impossible. The death of a parent, sibling, or friend at an early age may mean that a loved one was not able to be at the funeral or does not remember being there.

Perhaps it is a trip across relationships that makes being at a memorial service an impossibility. Strained or ended relationships, relationships that are not socially accepted, terminated pregnancies, or even suicides are all instances where a public appearance may not be an option. Sometimes loved ones just need a private time to say goodbye.

In all of these instances, and many others, loved ones can be encouraged to have a private service for the deceased. These services can take various forms and are as adaptable as the person. What follows are several suggestions that have been made to grieving loved ones.

Writing a Letter—Many times the grieving person simply needs to get their grief out, and writing a letter to the deceased is a good way to let the feelings flow and bring closure to this reality of the relationship even as the relationship is transformed. The person can then keep the letter, burn the letter in a fire, bury it in the ground, perhaps at a cemetery, or allow it to flow away on water in a stream, river, ocean, or lake. This is a good use of the elements in helping the person to heal.

Building a Fire—At times the grieving person is encouraged to build a fire, perhaps on a beach or waterfront, in an outside fire pit, or even in a fireplace at home. As the flames consume the wood, the grieving person is encouraged to allow the tears and laughter to come as they remember their loved one and say goodbye.

Swimming in a Pool of Water—Whether it is a swimming pool, the ocean, or a lake, the grieving loved one is encouraged to allow the healing properties of the water to wash away their grief. A variation is to shower in the privacy of home, allowing the stream of water to wash away the grief and the tears.

Raising a Toast—Toasting loved ones and telling stories and memories is always a good way to celebrate and to grieve. This might be a ritual better done in a small group, but it certainly could be done alone. It could become an annual ritual as well, on the birthday or the anniversary of the death, as a way to remember and to celebrate that life and relationship.

Flowers on the Water—Standing on a bridge over a slow-moving river, the grieving person may pluck the petals from a rose or other flower and let them drop into the water. With each petal the griever can recall a memory or say something to the deceased loved one.

Plant a Tree or a Garden—Bringing new life into this world is a way of allowing the grief to be transformed. Using the element of the earth, the grieving one is encouraged to plant a tree or a garden in the memory of their loved one. As the plants or tree grows, it can be a reminder of how grief is also being transformed.

Variations—There are many other things grieving persons can be encouraged to do to move their sadness from their hearts and into the world. The grieving should also be encouraged to create their own rituals to celebrate and commemorate. If a loved one does not want a grave or a marker, perhaps a bench might be created and dedicated to the loved one. Perhaps something could be done in the world to commemorate the deceased, such as gifts to a children's hospital, flowers to a nursing home, or donations to the agencies that took care of the loved one.

Ashes/Cremains—Sometimes these private rituals are centered around what to do with the cremated remains of a loved one. Again, any of these rituals can be adapted to include a time of releasing ashes to the elements. If there is a question as to where ashes can be spread, a quick search on the Internet can usually give the answer. Ashes can be spread on any private land with the permission of the owner. Ashes can also be spread on open flowing waters, though checking for local ordinances is usually best. Ashes may also be incorporated into various pieces of jewelry, art, and keepsakes. These too can become part of the private ceremony at the first time the piece is worn, unwrapped, or used.

Grieving Rituals Used in a Group Setting

The deathbed continuum may include bereavement, although this may not formally be within the scope of some chaplains' services. The following rituals are part of a six-week grief class that is loosely based on the seasons of a year. The classes incorporate a video series called *When Mourning Dawns.*[46] As each week progresses so does the year through the seasons. The class begins with an introductory session, which introduces the participants to the facilitators, each other, the video series, and what grief might look like for them.

Four weeks are organized around the seasons—autumn, winter, spring, summer—and how that season might reflect a season of grief. One week (usually placed between winter and spring) acknowledges holidays and grieving. It is also important to note that when the weeks turn to spring and summer, the facilitators are very cognizant and share with the participants that they may not be ready for this season yet. Participants are encouraged to listen with an open mind and heart and take with them what they can. Each week the class ends with some sort of ritual that both closes the session and also gives the participant a grounding in the Spiritual to take with them into the coming week. These rituals have had varying success over the years, but most participants find them helpful and say so on their evaluations at the end of the period.

First Week—Introduction

At the end of the first class a bowl of rocks that have been collected from local beaches is passed around. Each person is asked to take one and to listen to this story.

Naomi Rachel Remen in *Kitchen Table Wisdom*[47] tells the story that when she is sending a patient into chemotherapy or radiation treatments, she suggests that the patient have a dinner for her close friends and relatives. She then suggests that the patient tell those gathered what she is facing and that their support is really needed. Remen then suggests the patient pass around a rock and ask each person to put blessings, prayers, and well wishes into the rock. Then the patient is encouraged to carry the rock to treatment to remind them of this support.

Class participants are asked to begin passing their rocks around the circle. Each time a person gets a rock, they are asked to put their prayers, blessings, or well wishes into it. Though the owner may not be known, participants will know that the person shares their grief. And so the rocks go all the way around the circle with lots of love, blessings, and prayers. While the rocks are being passed, music is played and the facilitator keeps track of when the rocks have made the complete passage.

One participant was so moved by this activity and the surprising healing it brought to him that he wrote this poem titled "A Stone":

I've known the power of a single flame,
a candle
lighting up my soul
stilling fear
chasing loneliness away
But a stone?

Yes
prayed over,
blessed
with the love
and compassionate energy
of others
I am surprised
by a single stone
that accompanies me,
flowing with a
mountain size stream
of peace
and pleasure![48]

This ritual has also been adapted for many other occasions as well. Wedding participants sometimes have been asked to hold rocks, shells, pieces of beach glass, or old keys, putting well wishes in them for the couple and then returning the items to the couple. At a deathbed or any time someone is sick, family and friends could use a stuffed animal, a flower, or some other item, which could give the patient comfort and a reminder of the love that surrounds them. It has also been used with crystals or stones that were then taken into ordination interviews, certification committees, or other times when a person being evaluated needs to be reminded that they have the support of others.

Second Week—Autumn

At the end of the first week, participants are invited to bring with them a personal symbol—a small picture or memento of the loved one who has brought them to the class—the reason for their grief. There is an altar (small round table with a candle, rocks, and a flower) in the center of the room and the tables are arranged in a circle around it. Participants are told that in the second week they will be asked to tell about the picture or memento and why it is an important touchstone. They are also asked to leave the item with the facilitators for the duration of the classes.

As participants check in at the beginning of the second week (a ritual in itself that is followed every week) they are also asked to share what item they brought and why it is important to them. Though bringing the item and sharing are both voluntary, most of the time each person participates and is happy to do so.

At the end of the session, the facilitator invites the participants to bring the items forward to place them on the altar (or, if more practical, to hand the item to the facilitator, who places each person's item on the altar). They are invited to kiss, stroke, or just give the item a last look as they bring it up, as they will not see this item until the next class. The facilitator explains that the items will be on the altar each week to remind the class that loved ones have not completely left us.

Third Week—Winter

The third week is often quite emotional. The class has been together for three weeks and they are beginning to grasp the reality of their grief and that they are not alone. The material and images from the video series are also quite stark and real. Thus the ritual at the end of the third week is designed to bring hope and brightness.

The facilitator begins with a personal story of being prepared for the ravages of a season. This might mean having supplies for violent weather or having a snow kit in a car in case of being stuck in a blizzard. But almost all of these kits have a candle in them to dispel darkness and bring warmth and comfort.

On the altar—in addition to the one candle, rocks, flower, and items from the participants—is also a bowl of sand. Participants are each given a candle. The facilitator usually uses *Hanukkah* candles, but any candle of similar size can be used. The facilitator invites the participants to come forward and light their candle from the main candle and speak a word that gives them strength and/or comfort during the dark times. This word can be a value, a name, or even an activity. The participant then sticks the lit candle into the stand. While this goes on, some music is played in the background.

Once everyone has lit their candles and returned to their seats, the facilitator turns off the lights and comments on the power that their individual lights of strength and warmth have made in the dark room, and thus can do the same for them as they go through this week.

Fourth Week—Holidays

The fourth week curriculum has been about how to survive the holidays when one is grieving. The facilitators have defined the holidays as being any time that was special or sacred to the relationship between the grieving and the loved one. Thus a holiday can certainly mean Christmas and Thanksgiving (the "big ones") but can also be birthdays, anniversaries, or any other day that was special—Valentine's Day, Fourth of July, or Halloween.

To the altar has been added a candelabra or wreath with five candles surrounded by greenery, a few rocks, and the items from the participants. One candle has been burning throughout class. It is extinguished.

The facilitator passes out the text of the ritual called "Holiday Memorial" and asks for volunteers to read the five different pieces for the five candles. The facilitator can stand at the candelabra or wreath and light the candles or the individuals doing the reading can come forward. The text of the ceremony can be found in Appendix 4.

At the end of the ceremony, the facilitator reads the blessing "For Absence" by John O'Donohue[49], listed in Appendix 1. Participants are invited to use this ceremony any time they feel it would be helpful.

Fifth Week—Spring

At the end of the fifth (spring) week, the facilitator has set up a station with flower pots, potting soil, and some sort of future plant germinating item. This item is usually a bulb, but seeds can also be used, especially in later summer.

Participants are reminded that right now they may still feel like their grief is not at the springtime yet. They may still feel like a bulb that has yet to reach its full potential and bloom. But the facilitators make the promise that, like the bulb planted in the ground, which will bloom in the spring, their grief will also lead the way to new growth.

Participants are then invited to come up and plant a bulb to take home with them. The pot is really symbolic of the ground they should plant it in when they do get home. (Usually the pots are the kind that can simply be placed in the ground.) The facilitator should be near the planting station to help participants with the planting as they need it.

This is perhaps the ritual that is most often commented on years later when participants speak to the facilitator and explain that their bulb is still blooming each year, reminding them of their loved one.

Sixth Week—Summer and Going Forth

For two weeks prior to this class, facilitators have asked participants to begin considering bringing a food item to the final week's class. This food item should be something that reminds them of their loved one; it does not have to be elaborate. This item could be a favorite food, perhaps a food the participant could not eat because of the loved one, or even a food they have avoided or indulged in since the death. Participants are also asked to be ready to tell the story about their selection.

At the beginning of the sixth class, during the check-in time, the food items are placed on a table that has been set with a tablecloth, plates, and utensils. The participants are asked to explain what they brought and why they brought it. Once the group has finished speaking, the facilitator explains that eating a meal together symbolizes being a family and caring for each other. The facilitator then invites everyone to dish up some food and continue to talk and share stories.

This time of fellowship is an important ending to the six weeks of classes as it gives the participants an opportunity to celebrate their loved ones and each other.

Conclusion

"Did I do enough?" –
Realizing Presence is Most Important

The mother arrived at the door of my office in tears. Her daughter's brain tumor had taken too much out her daughter, and she was still under 10 years old. What had started as a headache had since torn this family apart with grief. Now the mother was crying, exhausted, and scared. "She just told me she wanted to go home. When I told her that it would be a few more days, she said, 'No Mom. Home. I want to go home.' She doesn't mean our house." As she dissolved into tears that would bring about acceptance, I realized how much wisdom can be found in a child facing her own death.

It has been the focus of this project not only to identify symbols and rituals that have the ability to connect to the Spiritual but also to show how these can in turn aid in helping a patient leave this world more grounded and aware of the spiritual reality that they are. Whether the symbols were traditionally-held elemental symbols, common objects from the person's life, favorite writings filled with wisdom, or sacred objects that they identify as connecting points, these symbols help the person feel a connection to the Spiritual and to the people who have gone before her. These symbols can be from the four elements, which have always held great spiritual value throughout the wisdom of human history. Using water, fire, earth, and air as part of the spiritual connection reminds the patient that their death is also part of the rhythm of life. When these symbols are combined into a ritual and shared with others in community or simply with those gathered, the patient realizes that her journey is not one she takes alone.

Symbols are also important touchstones for the family even after the death. If some symbol that was used at the deathbed or identified as important to the patient can be incorporated in a later ritual, then it can evoke feelings of connection to the patient and the Spiritual. That is why so many times particular poems or prayers are written on funeral programs, why the singing bowl can be used in both a bedside ritual and a memorial service, and why participants are asked to bring a memento to a grief class. These items serve, then, as bridging symbols along the deathbed continuum.

The rituals that were offered in this project were compiled from the many different times the chaplain has stood at a deathbed with a family who "just wanted something" but were not sure what they wanted. These rituals are offered as a starting point for chaplains and palliative spiritual care providers. Each part of each ritual can be taken separately or combined into new practices involving a few or many of the symbols described throughout this study. Consideration and awareness must always be given to the specific situation. The chaplain has to be careful not to overload the patient or the family. Brevity is often more comforting and accessible. A ten-minute ritual can be more effective than one that lasts a half hour in most cases.

Though there are many funeral resources on the market, many are based in a particular faith tradition. What is offered in this project is a framework/template of services when the family and chaplain need a place to start. Again, it is very important to ask the patient and/or family for input. Many times patients are unable to give input, but when they do, it should be observed to the extent practicable. Some believe that planning a memorial service is hard on a family, but the chaplain may embrace these experiences as a time to help the family begin the grieving process. Many families realize later, after planning a memorial service, that the process was a healing time for them, though they may not have recognized it at the time.

After the death, many loved ones struggle with what they self-describe as a "roller coaster of emotions," where they know they want to be happy for the fact that their loved one is no longer suffering, but they still miss the loved one deeply. A person might become sad and start to cry for no apparent reason while in a grocery store or other place unrelated to the deceased. The cacophony of emotions can lead to times of joy followed by guilt for being happy followed by times of depression. Alan Wolfelt refers to these times as "griefbursts." The grieving are encouraged to see these as not only expected, but as a right.[50] This is the right time to encourage the grieving to embrace the emotions and allow them to flow. This emotional connection can also help to connect them to the Spiritual, especially if they embrace the use of ritual.

This study has explored and expanded various rituals that can be used along the deathbed continuum, but it is important to return to the origins of this work and to connect to the broader spirituality that chaplains and palliative spiritual care providers are called on to embody when serving a wide spectrum of clients. It is appropriate to bring the focus back to the way the course of study has actually influenced the practice of this project. One course studying Comparative Mysticism began by discussing the "emic versus etic" ways of studying anything, but especially something as culturally specific as religion. [51] The *etic* stands on the outside and attempts to learn what he can from that vantage point. The *emic* feels it is best to delve into the society and learn from there. For this project the position of the *emic* seems to be in order. Even though the chaplain may not be Jewish, Pagan, or Buddhist, he has the responsibility to learn about other spiritualities as if they were his own. The inside view seems to be the most operational and functional and generally unavoidable, perhaps out of sheer necessity, as chaplains are thrust into contexts with minimal information and perhaps no personal or academic experience. This study sought to provide *emic* starting points for those engaged in this work and service.

This seems to be a more expansive and concurrently more inclusive way of experiencing the Spiritual as well. Wisdom says that humans cannot know the mind of God, yet in participating in the action of the

Spiritual, humans can begin to recognize the Spiritual in the world and thus help that Spiritual to be recognized by others. A concluding thought from Evelyn Underhill states:

> For them (the mystics) contemplation and action are not opposites but two interdependent forms of a life that is one. A life that rushes out to a passionate communion with the true and beautiful.[52]

"Did I do enough?" might be a question that still lingers in the mind of those who care. Though individuals may always wonder that, presence is an important part of any sacred time with another person. The hope is that the reader has understood that symbols and rituals can make any time of sadness or grief a sacred time.

Using rituals at the deathbed and through the grieving period does not guarantee mystical experiences for the patient or the family, but ritual is a pathway for the Spiritual. If chaplains and others can be instruments for the Spiritual to use to enter this world and to allow the dying a pathway from this existence, then they have taken that step from simply watching the experience to participating in the action of the Spiritual in both contemplation and action.

Readings and Blessings at the Deathbed

Nonreligious Readings

This first group of readings consist of poems and reflections taken from various traditions. These readings are generally not religious even though some of them might have an occasional mention of God or other sacred language. Some have been mentioned elsewhere in this project. Some are more appropriate for funerals and memorial services rather than at the bedside of a patient close to death.

Entering Death
by John O'Donohue
I pray that you will have the blessing
Of being consoled and sure about your death.

May you know in your soul
There is no need to be afraid.

When your time comes, may you have
Every blessing and strength you need.

May there be a beautiful welcome for you
In the home you are going to.

You are not going somewhere strange,
Merely back to the home you have never left.

May you live with compassion
And transfigure everything
Negative within and about you.

When you come to die,
May it be after a long life.

May you be tranquil
Among those who care for you.

May your going be sheltered
And your welcome assured.

May your soul smile
In the embrace
Of your Anam Cara.[53]

On the Death of the Beloved
by John O'Donohue

Though we need to weep your loss,
You dwell in that safe place in our hearts,
Where no storm or night or pain can reach you.

Your love was like the dawn
Brightening over our lives
Awakening beneath the dark
A further adventure of colour.

The sound of your voice
Found for us
A new music
That brightened everything.

Whatever you enfolded in your gaze
Quickened in the joy of its being;
You placed smiles like flowers
On the altar of the heart.
Your mind always sparkled
With wonder at things.

Though your days here were brief,
Your spirit was alive, awake, complete.

We look towards each other no longer
From the old distance of our names;
Now you dwell inside the rhythm of breath,
As close to us as we are to ourselves.

Though we cannot see you with outward eyes,
We know our soul's gaze is upon your face,
Smiling back at us from within everything
To which we bring our best refinement.

Let us not look for you only in memory,
Where we would grow lonely without you.
You would want us to find you in presence,
Beside us when beauty brightens,
When kindness glows
And music echoes eternal tones.

When orchids brighten the earth,
Darkest winter has turned to spring;
May this dark grief flower with hope
In every heart that loves you.

May you continue to inspire us:

To enter each day with a generous heart.
To serve the call of courage and love

Until we see your beautiful face again
In that land where there is no more separation,
Where all tears will be wiped from our mind,
And where we will never lose you again.[54]

For Absence
by John O'Donohue
May you know that absence is full
of tender presence and that
nothing is ever lost or forgotten.

May the absences in your life be full of
eternal echo.

May you sense around you the secret
Elsewhere which holds the presences
that have left your life.

May you be generous in your embrace of
loss.

May the sore of your grief turn into a well
of seamless presence.

May your compassion reach out to the ones
we never hear from and may you have
the courage to speak out for the excluded
ones.

May you become the gracious and
passionate subject of your own life.

May you not disrespect your mystery
through brittle words or false belonging.

May you be embraced by the Ground of All Being
in whom dawn and twilight are one and may
your longing inhabit its deepest dreams
within the shelter of the Great Belonging.[55]

Funeral Blues
by W. H. Auden
Stop all the clocks, cut off the telephone,
Prevent the dog from barking with a juicy bone,
Silence the pianos and with muffled drum
Bring out the coffin, let the mourners come.

Let aeroplanes circle moaning overhead
Scribbling on the sky the message He Is Dead,
Put crepe bows round the white necks of the public doves,
Let the traffic policemen wear black cotton gloves.

He was my North, my South, my East and West,
My working week and my Sunday rest,
My noon, my midnight, my talk, my song;
I thought that love would last for ever: I was wrong.

The stars are not wanted now: put out every one;
Pack up the moon and dismantle the sun;
Pour away the ocean and sweep up the wood.
For nothing now can ever come to any good.[56]

Desiderata
by Max Ehrmann
Go placidly amid the noise and the haste,
and remember what peace there may be in silence.
As far as possible, without surrender,
be on good terms with all persons.

Speak your truth quietly and clearly; and listen to others,
even to the dull and the ignorant; they too have their story.

Avoid loud and aggressive persons; they are vexatious
to the spirit. If you compare yourself with others,
you may become vain or bitter, for always
there will be greater and lesser persons than yourself.

Enjoy your achievements as well as your plans.
Keep interested in your own career, however humble;
it is a real possession in the changing fortunes of time.

Exercise caution in your business affairs, for the world is full of trickery.
But let this not blind you to what virtue there is;
many persons strive for high ideals,
and everywhere life is full of heroism.

Be yourself. Especially do not feign affection.
Neither be cynical about love; for in the face of all aridity and
disenchantment,
it is as perennial as the grass.

Take kindly the counsel of the years,
gracefully surrendering the things of youth.

Nurture strength of spirit to shield you in sudden misfortune.
But do not distress yourself with dark imaginings.
Many fears are born of fatigue and loneliness.

Beyond a wholesome discipline, be gentle with yourself.
You are a child of the universe no less than the trees and the stars;
you have a right to be here.

And whether or not it is clear to you,
no doubt the universe is unfolding as it should.
Therefore be at peace with God,
whatever you conceive Him to be.

And whatever your labors and aspirations,
in the noisy confusion of life, keep peace in your soul.
With all its sham, drudgery and broken dreams,
it is still a beautiful world. Be cheerful. Strive to be happy.[57]

A Reflection on an Autumn Day
Author unknown
I took up a handful of grain and let it slip flowing through my fingers,
and I said to myself

This is what it is all about. There is no longer any room for pretense. At harvest time the essence is revealed—the straw and chaff are set aside, they have done their job. The grain alone matters—sacks of pure gold.

So it is when a person dies the essence of that person is revealed. At the moment of death a person's character stands out happy for the person who has forged it well over the years. Then it will not be the great achievement that will matter, nor how much money or possessions a person has amassed. These, like the straw and the chaff, will be left behind. It is what he has made of himself that will matter. Death can take away from us what we have, but it cannot rob us of who we are.[58]

The Serenity Prayer
by Reinhold Niebuhr
God grant me the serenity
to accept the things I cannot change;
courage to change the things I can;
and wisdom to know the difference.
Living one day at a time; Enjoying one moment at a time;
Accepting hardships as the pathway to peace;
Taking, as He did, this sinful worldas it is, not as I would have it;
Trusting that He will make all things right if I surrender to His Will;
That I may be reasonably happy in this life
and supremely happy with Him Forever in the next. Amen.[59]

Remember Me
Author unknown
To the living, I am gone.
To the sorrowful, I will never return.
To the angry, I was cheated,
But to the happy, I am at peace,
And to the faithful, I have never left.
I cannot be seen, but I can be heard.

So as you stand upon a shore, gazing at a beautiful sea—remember me.
As you look in awe at a mighty forest and its grand majesty—remember me.
As you look upon a flower and admire its simplicity—remember me.
Remember me in your heart, your thoughts, and your memories of the times we loved, the times we cried, the times we fought, the times we laughed.
For if you always think of me, I will have never gone.[60]

from *Walden*
by Henry David Thoreau
I went to the woods because I wished to live deliberately, to front only the essential facts of life, and see if I could not learn what it had to teach, and not, when I came to die, discover that I had not lived. I did not wish to live what was not life, living is so dear; nor did I wish to practise resignation, unless it was quite necessary. I wanted to live deep and suck out all the marrow of life.[61]

Prayer of Faith
Author unknown
We trust that beyond absence there is a presence.
That beyond the pain there can be healing.
That beyond the brokenness there can be wholeness.
That beyond the anger there may be peace.
That beyond the hurting there may be forgiveness.
That beyond the silence there may be the word.
That beyond the word there may be understanding.
That through understanding there is love.[62]

Do Not Stand on my Grave and Weep
attributed to Mary Frye

Do not stand on my grave and weep;
I am not there. I do not sleep.
I am a thousand winds that blow.
I am the diamond's glint on snow.
I am the sunlight on ripened grain.
I am the gentle autumn's rain.
When you awaken in the morning's hush,
I am the swift uplifting rush of quiet birds in circled flight.
I am the soft stars that shine at night.
Do not stand at my grave and cry;
I am not there. I did not die.[63]

For This We Give Thanks
by Michael Leunig

Dear God,
We struggle, we grow weary, we grow tired.
We are exhausted, we are distressed, we despair.
We give up, we fall down, we let go.
We cry. We are empty, we grow calm, we are ready.
We wait quietly.
A small, shy truth arrives.
Arrives from without and within.
Arrives and is born.
Simple, steady, clear.
Like a mirror, like a bell, like a flame.
Like rain in summer.
A precious truth arrives and is born within us.
Within our emptiness.
We accept it, we observe it, we absorb it.
We surrender to our bare truth.
We are nourished, we are changed.
We are blessed. We rise up.
For this we give thanks.
Amen[64]

Absolutely Clear
by Hafiz

Don't surrender your loneliness
So quickly.
Let it cut more deep.

Let it ferment and season you
As few human
Or even divine ingredients can

Something missing in my heart tonight
Has made my eyes so soft,
My voice
So tender

My need of God
Absolutely
Clear.[65]

Let Evening Come
by Jane Kenyon

Let the light of late afternoon
shine through chinks in the barn, moving
up the bales as the sun moves down.

Let the cricket take up chafing
as a woman takes up her needles
and her yarn. Let evening come.

Let dew collect on the hoe abandoned
in long grass. Let the stars appear
and the moon disclose her silver horn.

Let the fox go back to its sandy den.
Let the wind die down. Let the shed
go black inside. Let evening come.

To the bottle in the ditch, to the scoop
in the oats, to air in the lung
let evening come.

Let it come, as it will, and don't
be afraid. God does not leave us
comfortless, so let evening come.[66]

Sufi Prayer for the Dying
by Rumi

On the day I die, when I'm being carried
toward the grave, don't weep. Don't say,
He's gone! He's gone. Death has nothing
to do with going away. The sun sets and
the moon sets, but they're not gone.
Death is a coming together. The tomb
looks like a prison, but it's really
release into union. The human seed goes
down in the ground like a bucket into
the well where Joseph is. It grows and
comes up full of some unimagined beauty.
Your mouth closes here and immediately
opens with a shout of joy there.[67]

Testament
by Anne Morrow Lindbergh

But how can I live without you?—she cried.

I left all the world to you when I died:
Beauty of earth and air and sea;
Leap of a swallow or a tree;
Kiss of rain and wind's embrace;
Passion of storm and winter's face;
Touch of feather, flower, and stone;
Chiselled line of branch or bone;

Flight of stars, night's caravan;
Song of crickets—and of man—
All these I put in my testament,
All these I bequeathed you when I went.

But how can I see them without your eyes
Or touch them without your hand?
How can I hear them without your ear,
Without your heart, understand?

These too, these too,
I leave to you![68]

Grief Never Ends
Author Unknown
Grief never ends...
But it changes.
It's a passage, not a place to stay.
Grief is not a sign of weakness, nor a lack of faith....
It is the price of love.[69]

Though the following poems are not reprinted here, these are poems that a chaplain might find useful in rituals. Information on each can be found in the bibliography. Texts of these poems can generally be found online.

- "In Blackwater Woods" from *American Primitive* by Mary Oliver.
- "When Death Comes" from *New and Selected Poems, Vol. 1* by Mary Oliver.
- "Wild Geese" from *New and Selected Poems, Vol. 1* by Mary Oliver.
- "Many Winters" from *Many Winters: Prose and Poetry of the Pueblos* by Nancy Wood.
- "For Joel at 94" from *Reduced to Joy* by Mark Nepo.

Readings, Prayers, and Blessings from Specific Religious Traditions

Many of these can be used for traditions beyond those they were written for. The chaplain does not need to feel he cannot use a prayer outside of that tradition, but he should be aware of the language that is used.

Prayer at the Death of a Loved One
by Edward Hays
Help us, Compassionate God, to let Your ancient and eternal song of death and life be played out in each of us, as we live out our faith that death is but a doorway that opens unto a greater and fuller expression of life, that opens to a final union with You who are life! Blessed are You, Lord of Life, who alone knows the hour of our death and ultimate union with You. Blessed are You, Lord our God, whose messenger is death. Amen [70]

Christian (Lutheran) Prayer for a Sick Person
Blessed Lord, we ask your loving care and protection for those who are sick in body, mind, or spirit and who desire our prayers. Take from them all fears and help them put their trust in you, that they may feel your strong arms around them. Touch them with your renewing love, that they may know wholeness in you and glorify your name; through Jesus Christ our Lord. Amen[71]

Christian (Methodist) Prayer for a Dying Person
Gracious God, you are nearer than hands or feet, closer than breathing. Sustain with your presence our brother/sister (NAME). Help him/her now to trust in your goodness and claim your promise of life everlasting. Cleanse him/her of all sin and remove all burdens. Grant him/her the sure joy of your salvation, through Jesus Christ our Lord. Amen[72]

Praising the Bodhisattva of Compassion (Buddhist)
The Nectar of Compassion is seen on the willow branch held by the Bodhisattva. A single

drop of this nectar is enough to bring life to the
Ten Directions of the Cosmos. May all afflictions
of this world disappear totally and may
this place of practice be completely purified by
the Bodhisattva's Nectar of Compassion.
Homage to the Bodhisattva Who Refreshes
the Earth.

From deep understanding, the flower of great
eloquence blooms: the Bodhisattva standing
majestically on the waves of birth and death,
free from all afflictions. Her compassion eliminates
all sickness, even that thought of as incurable.
Her light sweeps away all obstacles and
dangers. The willow branch in her hand, once
it is waved, reveals countless Buddha lands.
Her lotus flower, when it blooms, becomes a
multitude of practice centers. I bow to her. I
see her true presence in the here and the now.
I offer her the incense of my heart. May the
Bodhisattva of Deep Listening touch us with
her Great Compassion.
Homage to Bodhisattva Avalokiteshvara
[two bells].[73]

Hindu Prayer for Peace
From *The Vedas*, trans. Raimundo Panniker
May there be peace in the higher regions; may there be peace in the
firmament;
may there be peace on earth.
May the waters flow peacefully; may the herbs and plants grow peacefully;
may all the divine powers bring unto us peace.
The supreme Lord is peace.
May we all be in peace, peace, and only peace; and may that peace come
unto each of us.
Shanti (peace) Shanti—Shanti![74]

Hindu Upanishads
Adapted from the Hindu Upanishads by Satish Kumar
Lead me from death to life,
from falsehood to truth.
Lead me from despair to hope,
from fear to trust.
Lead me from hate to love,
from war to peace.
Let peace fill our heart, our world, our universe.
Peace, peace, peace.[75]

Mantra of Avalokiteshvara (Jewel Mantra)
Oṃ maṇi padme hūṃ[76] (ancient Sanskrit mantra)

Mi Sheberakh (Jewish Prayer for Healing)
May the One who blessed our ancestors—
Patriarchs Abraham, Isaac, and Jacob,
Matriarchs Sarah, Rebecca, Rachel, and Leah—
bless and heal the one who is ill:
_____ son/daughter of _____ .
May the Holy Blessed One
overflow with compassion upon him/her,
to restore him/her,
to heal him/her,
to strengthen him/her,
to enliven him/her.
The One will send him/her, speedily,
a complete healing—
healing of the soul and healing of the body—
along with all the ill,
among the people of Israel and all humankind,
soon,
speedily,
without delay,
and let us all say: Amen![77]

Shema
Sh'ma Yisra'eil Adonai Eloheinu Adonai echad.
Hear, Israel, the Lord is our G-d, the Lord is One.[78]

El Maley Rachamim (Jewish Prayer at Time of Death)
G-d full of mercy who dwells on high
Grant perfect rest on the wings of Your Divine Presence
In the lofty heights of the holy and pure
who shine as the brightness of the heavens
to the soul of _____
who has gone to his/her eternal rest
as all his/her family and friends
pray for the elevation of his/her soul.
May his/her resting place be in the Garden of Eden.
Therefore, the Master of mercy will care for him/her
under the protection of His wings for all time
And bind his/her soul in the bond of everlasting life.
G-d is his inheritance and he/her will rest in peace
and let us say Amen. [79]

Chasidic Teaching
We see our reflection in water only when we bend close to it. So too
your heart must lean down to another's. Then it will see itself in the
other's heart.

Song of a Man About to Die in a Strange Land (Native American Prayer) from the Ojibway Tribe
If I die here
In a strange land,
If I die
In a land not my own,
Nevertheless, the thunder
The rolling thunder
Will take me home.
If I die here, the wind,
The wind rushing over the prairie

The wind will take me home.
The wind and the thunder,
They are the same everywhere,
What does it matter, then,
If I die here in a strange land?[80]

Pagan/Wicca Prayer at Time of Death
by Crimson Peaceful Wolf

Time has passed, the Wheel has turned.
It is time for you [person's name] to move on.
You will walk hand in hand with the Lord and Lady
and with your ancestors who came before you.
Great Mother, welcome [name of person]
back into your womb.
And Great Father welcome [him/her] back
into your divine instruction.
Let [him/her] come to you and
know that [s/he] has been blessed
by your gracious gift of Life.
Let [him/her] come into your Divine Love,
and let [him/her] know
that [s/he] has left behind a life of legacy,
that [s/he] shall be remembered and loved.
As [s/he] enters your world,
wrap [him/her] in your loving arms,
and welcome [him/her] back home.
Let [him/her] speak to the Ancient Ones
to learn the greater mysteries
that lie beyond the veil.
Give [him/her] the strength to take these final steps,
and allow [him/her] to do so with peace and dignity.
Those of us left behind
shall indeed mourn [his/her] death,
but we shall also know
that [his/her] Soul and Spirit
is coming back

to Holy Mother and Holy Father,
and that [s/he] shall be made whole again.
We shall cry, but we shall also laugh,
for we shall celebrate the Life
that had been given to [person's name.]
And let [him/her] also know
that as we now merry part,
that we shall also merry meet again.
And we now, with these candles {light candles}
respect the flame of [person's name]'s life,
and though these candle flames shall die out,
we know that [person's name] shall live on,
and [his/her] flame shall never cease to burn,
and we also know that [s/he] shall be reborn anew.
Take [him/her] by the hand and
guide [him/her] back into your heart,
for this is what is right and just.
Let [him/her] walk unerringly
down the path that leads to your Love.
This is our will and so mote it be.
Amen and Amen.[81]

Baha'i Prayer
from 'Abdu'l-Bahá

O God! Refresh and gladden my spirit. Purify my heart. Illumine my powers. I lay all my affairs in Thy hand. Thou art my Guide and my Refuge. I will no longer be sorrowful and grieved; I will be a happy and joyful being.
O God! I will no longer be full of anxiety, nor will I let trouble harass me. I will not dwell on the unpleasant things of life.
O God! Thou art more friend to me than I am to myself. I dedicate myself to Thee, O Lord.[82]

What follow are variations of three psalms, 23, 91, and 121, which are well-known readings used at the deathbed and at funerals. As these examples show, psalms can be adjusted for use in various instances and various traditions. Many other variations can be found in books and online.

Psalm 23 (NKJV)

The Lord *is* my shepherd;
I shall not want.
He makes me to lie down in green pastures;
He leads me beside the still waters.
He restores my soul;
He leads me in the paths of righteousness
For His name's sake.

Yea, though I walk through the valley of the shadow of death,
I will fear no evil;
For You *are* with me;
Your rod and Your staff, they comfort me.
You prepare a table before me in the presence of my enemies;
You anoint my head with oil;
My cup runs over.

Surely goodness and mercy shall follow me
All the days of my life;
And I will dwell in the house of the Lord
Forever.[83]

Psalm 23
adapted by Nan Merrill

O my Beloved, you are my shepherd,
　　　I shall not want;
You bring me to green pastures
　　　　　for rest
　　　and lead me beside still waters,
　　　　　renewing my spirit,
　　　You restore my soul.
You lead me in the path of
　　　　　goodness
　　　to follow Love's way.

Even though I walk through
     the valley of the shadow and
        of death,
   I am not afraid;
For You are ever with me;
     your rod and your staff
        they guide me,
     they give me strength
        and comfort.

You prepare a table before me
     in the presence of all my fears;
        you bless me with oil,
        my cup overflows.
Surely goodness and mercy will
     follow me
     all the days of my life;
and I shall dwell in the heart
     of the Beloved
        forever.[84]

Psalm 91:1-2, 9-16

You who live in the shelter of the Most High,
     who abide in the shadow of the Almighty,
will say to the LORD, "My refuge and my fortress;
     my God, in whom I trust."
...Because you have made the LORD your refuge,
     the Most High your dwelling place,
no evil shall befall you,
     no scourge come near your tent.

For he will command his angels concerning you
     to guard you in all your ways.
On their hands they will bear you up,
     so that you will not dash your foot against a stone.

You will tread on the lion and the adder,
      the young lion and the serpent you will trample under foot.

Those who love me, I will deliver;
      I will protect those who know my name.
When they call to me, I will answer them;
      I will be with them in trouble,
      I will rescue them and honor them.
With long life I will satisfy them,
      and show them my salvation.[85]

Psalm 91
adapted by Nan Merrill
Those who dwell in the shelter of
      Infinite Light,
    who abide in the wings of
      Infinite Love,
Will raise their voices in praise:
      "My refuge and my strength,
      In You alone will I trust."
For you deliver me from the webs
      of fear,
      from all that separates and divides;
You protect me as an eagle shields
      its young.
      Your faithfulness is sure, like
        an arrow set upon the mark.
I will not fear the shadows of the night,
      nor the confusion that comes
        by day,
Nor the dreams that awaken me from
      sleep,
      nor the daily changes that
        life brings.

housand may deride this
radical trust,
ten thousand laugh as I seek
to do your Will,
Yet will I surrender myself to You,
abandoning myself into your Hands
without reserve.

For You have sent your angels to
watch over me,
to guide me in all of your ways.
In their hands they will bear me up,
lest I dash my foot against
a stone.
Though I walk among those who
roar like the lion,
or are as stealthy as the adder,
in your strength will I be saved.

"Because you cleave to Me in love,
I will deliver you;
I will protect you who
call upon my Name.
When you call to Me, I will answer you;
I will be with you in times
of trouble.
I will rescue you and
reverence your life.
All through the years will I dwell
in your heart,
as Loving Companion Presence,
forever."[86]

Psalm 121

I lift up my eyes to the hills—
from where will my help come?

My help comes from the Lord,
who made heaven and earth.

He will not let your foot be moved;
 he who keeps you will not slumber.

He who keeps Israel
 will neither slumber nor sleep.

The Lord is your keeper;
the Lord is your shade at your right hand.

The sun shall not strike you by day,
nor the moon by night.

The Lord will keep you from all evil;
he will keep your life.

The Lord will keep
your going out and your coming in
from this time on and forevermore.[87]

Psalm 121
adapted by Nan Merrill

My heart's eyes behold your
                    Divine Glory!
          From whence does my help come?
My help comes from You,
          who created heaven and earth.

You strengthen and uphold me,
          You, who are ever by my side.
Behold! You who watch over the
                    nations
          will see all hearts Awaken
                    to the Light.

For You are the Great Counselor;
>   You dwell within all hearts,
>   that we might respond to the
>   Universal Heart—
Like the sun, that nourishes us by day,
>   like the stars that guide the
>   wayfarer at night.
In You we shall not be afraid of
>   the darkness, for
>   You are the Light of our life.
May You keep us in our going out
>   and our coming in
>   from this time forth and
>   forevermore.[88]

Music at the Deathbed

Music is highly personal and may reflect many different traditions. Consistent with the theme in this study, the chaplain surveys the environment, asks guiding questions, and simply asks for input. The patient or family may be able to make suggestions. Many times the family may have music playing for a patient. Take note of what is playing and the affect it is having on the patient. At times family members may look to the chaplain for suggestions. The recommendations included below represent a sample.

Stringed instruments—live or recorded—are usually calming in time of distress and death. One in particular that seems appropriate is called "Late Winter, Early Spring (When Everybody Goes to Mexico)" by John Denver on his *Rocky Mountain High* album.

Classical instrumentals that can play in the background:

- Rachmaninoff's *For a Rainy Day*
- *Piano Nocturnes* by Frederic Chopin—inspiring reflection, can vary in intensity. *Opus 9 No. 2, Andante*, is a familiar example.
- *Adagio for Strings*—Samuel Barber
- *Nimrod from Enigma Variations*—Edward Elgar
- Pachelbel's *Canon in D*

There are many hymns in the Christian tradition that are appropriate to be played at the deathbed or funeral services. This list includes hymns/

spirituals. The family/chaplain should especially consider using songs sung by the person's favorite artist:

- "The Day Is Past and Gone" by Aretha Franklin
- "Peace Like a River" by Paul Simon
- "Down to the River to Pray" and "A Living Prayer" by Alison Krauss
- "I'll Fly Away" by Johnny Cash
- "How Great Thou Art" and "You'll Never Walk Alone" by Elvis Presley
- "Amazing Grace" written by John Newton (various recordings are available)

Taize is a form of music based in the Christian tradition, but its rhythm and pace make it appropriate in many situations. Listed below are some pieces available as vocal and instrumental:

- *"Nada te turbe"*
- *"Ubi Caritas"*
- *"Gloria…et in terra pax"*
- *"Confitemini Domino"*
- *"Dona Nobis Pacem Domino"*
- "Stay With Me"
- "Jesus, Remember Me"

Choral music can also be quieting and may be familiar to the patient. Much choral music is based in the Christian tradition but may be appropriate for many. Listed are just a few more widely known pieces:

- "How Lovely Is Thy Dwelling Place" from *Requiem* by Brahms
- "In Paradisum," "Pie Jesu," "Agnus Dei" from *Requiem* by Faure
- "Gaelic Blessing (Deep Peace)" by John Rutter, performed by the Cambridge Singers
- "Jesus Is Calling" by Aaron David Miller
- "We Shall Walk through the Valley in Peace," arr. Moses Hogan
- "Psalm 23—For My Mother" by Bobby McFerrin (chant-like with feminine pronouns)

- Many requiems by Faure, Webber, and Rutter are quieter. Some that are listed as requiems may be more energetic and not as appropriate.

Buddhist chants—live or recorded—can bring calm and help prepare loved ones for death. If the patient has another religious/spiritual background, the chaplain can help the family find appropriate music. Here is a list of early sacred music/chants (Gregorian, Buddhist, other cultures):

- *Vision*—Hildegard von Bingen
- *Lost in Meditation*—Meditative Gregorian Chants
- *Angels and Saints at Ephesus*—Benedictines of Mary Queen of Apostles
- *The Essence*—Gayatri Mantra by Deva Premal (there is even a two-hour version on YouTube)

One collection of music seeks to combine many different traditions in various pieces, all of which seem to be appropriate for use at the deathbed. The album *Unspeakable Grace* by Gary Malkin is a project that spans beyond religion into common spirituality.

If the family is having difficulty deciding on what might be helpful, suggest they play music without words in a gentle instrumental style. Many music services offer channels with names such as "Soundscapes," "Zen Garden," or "New Age." These are also appropriate to play in the background while a ritual is being performed.

New age type music that is "rhythmless" (has no discernable beat) is decades old and even on Pandora or TV channels. Here are some suggestions:

- *Music for Transition*—touching deep with music
- Michael Sweeney—*Ancient Voices*—Drums, flutes and other instruments blend "with the echoes of ancestral voices from long ago."
- R. Carlos Nakai and others—*Feather, Stone and Light*— Sounds of nature "bring forth a music born and rooted in the Sonoran desert."
- Paul Baker—*The Tranquil Harp*—relaxing Celtic harp improvisation

- Carlos Nakai—Native American Flute
- Paul Winter albums—*Sun Singer, Misae Gaia, Canyon*, and several others
- Michael Hoppé and Tim Wheater—*The Yearning*—alto flute

Consider using national anthems for veterans and patients who had grown up in other countries. "Consider" is the key word here. Not all veterans would find these hymns comforting and not all immigrants to another country want to be reminded of the country they left. As always, the chaplain should ask the patient and family before assuming a piece of music would be comforting.

There is also the possibility that the patient might appreciate seasonal music, especially Christmas music. One elderly lady would play Christmas music even in the middle of summer. She said it always reminded her of happier times as a child.

Following are songs that have been used in memorial services over the years. This is not an extensive list, especially as patients may have particular songs that have meaning for them. Again, talking with family members or patients is the best way to find songs that are meaningful.

- "Sissy's Song" by Alan Jackson
- "Sand and Water" by Beth Nielsen Chapman
- "For Good" from the musical *Wicked*
- "Take Me Home" by Lisbeth Scott from the soundtrack *True Blood*
- "You Light Up My Life" by Debby Boone
- "You Raise Me Up" by Josh Groban
- "When I Get Where I am Going" by Brad Paisley and Dolly Parton
- "Balm of Gilead" by Sweet Honey and the Rock
- "Somewhere Over the Rainbow" by Israel Kamakawiwo'ole, aka "Iz"
- "Hymn for the Departed" by Dave Thomas Junior
- "Seasons of Love" from the musical *Rent*
- "Without You" from the musical *Rent*
- "'Cause of You" by Vicki Genfan
- "Danny Boy" written by Frederic Weatherly

- "I Was Here" by Beyoncé
- "Let Her Go" by Passenger
- "One Sweet Day" by Mariah Carey and Boyz II Men
- "In the Arms of An Angel" by Sarah McLachlan
- "I Will Remember You" by Sarah McLachlan
- "The Wings That Fly Us Home" by John Denver
- "My Heart Will Go On" by Celine Dion

APPENDIX 3

Beyond the Final Breath
Nursing Care at the Time of Death—
A Bathing and Honoring Practice

If the body is to be bathed, the nurse or family member is encouraged to say each of these blessings as that body part is bathed. If bathing is not possible, the nurse or family member can alternatively use oil, water, or touch to honor each body part as the blessing is recited.

Honoring Words

- We honor (name's) hair that the wind has played with
- We honor (name's) brow that have been the birthplace of her/ his thoughts
- We honor (name's) eyes that have looked on us with love and viewed the beauty of the earth
- We honor (name's) nostrils, that gateway of her/his breath
- We honor (name's) ears that listened for our voices
- We honor (name's) shoulders that have borne burdens and strengths
- We honor (name's) heart that has loved us
- We honor (name's) arms that have embraced us

- We honor (name's) hands that have held our hands and have done so many things in this life
- We honor (name's) legs that carried him/her into places of new challenge
- We honor (name's) feet that have walked his/her own path through life

We give thanks for the gifts that (name) has given us in this lifetime. Thanks for the abilities, the love, the care and even the human struggles of (name's) life. We give thanks for the memories that we created together. We have been honored to be part of (name's) life.[89]

APPENDIX 4

Holiday Memorial

BY SHERRY L. WILLIAMS-WHITE

For this ceremony, place five candles around a simple wreath, which you may wish to place on a table or fireplace mantel. As you light each candle this year, you may create a new ritual that will become a lasting tradition. We hope this memorial will help you honor your loved one.

As we light these five candles in honor of you, we light one for our grief, one for our courage, one for our memories, one for our love, and one for our hope.

This candle represents our grief. The pain of losing you is intense. It reminds us of the depth of our love for you.

This candle represents our courage—to confront our sorrow, to comfort each other, and to change our lives.

This candle is in your memory—the times we laughed, the times we cried, the times we were angry with each other, the silly things you did, and the caring and joy you gave us.

This candle is the light of love. We cherish the special place in our hearts that will always be reserved for you. We thank you for the gift your living brought to each of us.

And this candle is the light of hope. It reminds us of love and memories of you that are ours forever. May the glow of the flame be our source of hopefulness now and forever. We love you.

If possible, allow the candles to burn down while you share a meal of celebration of life, sharing stories and happy memories. [90]

Bibliography

Asimov, Nanette. "Stanford Gets a Chaplain for Atheists." *San Francisco Gate* (December 12, 2012). Accessed November 22, 2014. http://www.sfgate.com/news/article/Stanford-gets-a-chaplain-for-atheists-4139991.php.

Auden, W. H. *Selected Poems*. Edited Edward Mendelson. Expanded 2nd ed. New York: Vintage Books, 2007.

Austin, Mary. *The American Rhythm*. Santa Fe: Sunstone Press, 2003.

Awn, Peter. *Comparative Mysticism*. Edited by Steven Katz. Oxford: Oxford University Press, 2013.

Beliefnet. "Uplifting Prayers—Serenity Prayer." Accessed January 26, 2016. http://www.beliefnet.com/Prayers/Protestant/Addiction/Serenity-Prayer.aspx.

———. "Uplifting Prayers—El Maley Rachamim." Accessed February 15, 2016. http://www.beliefnet.com/Prayers/Judaism/Death/El-Maley-Rachamim.aspx?q=Shine.

Bell, Catherine. *Ritual Theory, Ritual Practice*. New York: Oxford University Press, 2009.

Braestrup, Kate. *Here If You Need Me*. New York: Back Bay Books, 2007.

Campbell, Joseph. *Flight of the Wild Gander: Explorations in the Mythological Dimension: Selected Essays, 1944-1968*. Novato, CA: New World Library, 2002.

Clarke, Jim. *Creating Rituals: A New Way of Healing for Everyday Life*. New York: Paulist Press, 2011.

Chauvet, Louis-Marie. *Symbol and Sacrament: A Sacramental Reinterpretation of Christian Existence*. Translated by Patrick

Madigan, SJ, and Madeleine Beaumont. Collegeville, MN: The Liturgical Press, 1995.

Cunningham, Scott. *Earth, Air, Fire & Water*. St. Paul: Llewellyn Publications, 1999.

Dewey, John. *A Common Faith*. New Haven: Yale University Press, 1934.

Ehrmann, Max. *Desiderata*. Wayland, MA: Bell & Son publishing, LLC, 1927.

Eliade, Mircea. *Images and Symbols: Studies in Religious Symbolism*. Translated by Philip Mairet. Princeton NJ: Princeton University Press, 1991.

———. *Patterns in Comparative Religion*. Translated by Rosemary Sheed. Lincoln, NE: First Bison Printing, 1996.

Friends Alternative Funerals. "Pagan Rituals." Accessed May 11, 2015. http://www.friendsaf.com/pagan-rituals/.

Funeral Helper. "Remember Me." Accessed January 25, 2016. http://funeralhelper.org/remember-me-in-your-heart-unknown-remembrance.html.

Furey, Robert J. *The Joy of Kindness*. New York: Crossroad, 1993.

Gerdner, Linda A. "Use of Individualized Music by Trained Staff and Family: Translating Research into Practice," *Journal of Gerontological Nursing* 31, no. 6 (June 2005): 22-30.

A Good Dying. "Islamic Prayers for the Dying." Accessed January 26, 2016. http://www.a-good-dying.com/islamic-prayers.html.

———. "Pagan and Wiccan Prayers for the Dying." Accessed January 26, 2016. http://www.a-good-dying.com/wiccan-prayers.html.

Hafiz. *The Subject Tonight is Love: 60 Wild and Sweet Poems of Hafiz*. Translated by Daniel Ladinsky. New York: Penguin Compass, 1996.

Hanh, Thich Nhat. *Plum Village Chanting and Recitation Book*. Berkeley, CA: Parallax Press, 2000.

Edward Hay, "Prayer at the Death of a Loved One." Holistic-Online.com. Prayer & Spirituality. Accessed November 22, 2014. http://1stholistic.com/spl_prayers/prayer_prayer-at-the-death-of-loved-one.htm.

Huffington Post Healthy Living. "Sing Your Prayers: An Interview with Bobby McFerrin." Accessed May 11, 2015. http://www.huffingtonpost.com/omega-institute-for-holistic-studies/bobby-mcferrin_b_1582043.html.

Inspiration Online. "Grief Never Ends." Accessed February 15, 2016, http://inspirationonline.com/2014/03/grief-never-ends/.

Jacobs, Martha R. *A Clergy Guide to End-of-Life Issues.* Cleveland, OH; The Pilgrim Press, 2010.

Joseph, Judith C. *Responding with Compassion.* Newtown PA: JCJoseph, Ltd., 2008.

Kabat-Zinn, Jon. *Coming to Our Senses: Healing Ourselves and the World through Mindfulness.* New York: Hyperion Books, 2005.

Kenyon, Jane. *Collected Poems.* St. Paul: Graywolf Press, 2005.

Krammer, Kenneth. *The Sacred Art of Dying.* New York: Paulist Press, 1988.

Leunig, Michael. *A Common Prayer.* North Blackburn, Victoria, AU: Collins Dove, 1990.

Lindbergh, Anne Morrow. *The Unicorn and Other Poems.* New York: Pantheon Books, 1956.

Lipp, Deborah. *The Elements of Ritual.* St. Paul: Llewellyn Publications, 2003.

McFerrin, Bobby. "The 23rd Psalm. From *Medicine Music,* 1990. EMI.

McKenna, Megan, and Tony Cowan. *Keepers of the Story.* Maryknoll, NY: Orbis Books, 1997.

Merrill, Nan. *Psalms for Praying.* New York: The Continuum International Publishing Group, 1996.

Miller, James E. *When Mourning Dawns: Living Your Way Fully Through the Seasons of Your Grief—The DVD.* Fort Wayne, IN: Willowgreen Inc., 2000.

Muslim Funeral Services Ltd. "The Ghusl Procedure." Accessed May 11, 2015. http://www.mfs.asn.au/ghusl--burial-steps.html.

"My Jewish Learning." Accessed January 26, 2016. http://www.myjewishlearning.com/texts/Liturgy_and_Prayers/Siddur_Prayer_Book/Torah_Service/Prayer_for_the_Sick.shtml.

Natural Endings. "Funeral Poetry." Accessed January 25, 2016. http://www.naturalendings.co.uk/funeral-poetry/.

Nepo, Mark. *Reduced to Joy.* Berkeley: Viva Editions, 2013.

Occasional Services: A Companion to the Lutheran Book of Worship. Minneapolis: Augsburg Publishing House, 1997.

O'Donohue, John. *Anam Cara.* New York: HarperCollins, 1997.

————. *To Bless the Space Between Us.* New York: Doubleday, 2008.

O'Neill, Jerry R. *Peach, Limestone, and Green* (Bloomington, IN: West Bow Press, 2015.

Oliver, Mary. *American Primitive.* Boston: Little, Brown & Co., 1983.

————. *New and Selected Poems, Vol. 1.* Boston: Beacon Press, 1992.

Pew Research Center. "Many Americans Mix Multiple Faiths." Accessed May 11, 2015. http://www.pewforum.org/2009/12/09/many-americans-mix-multiple-faiths/.

Remen, Rachel Naomi. *Kitchen Table Wisdom.* New York: Riverhead Books, 1996.

Reverend Blue Sky. "Readings for a Funeral." Accessed February 15, 2016. https://revbluesky.wordpress.com/readings/readings-for-a-funeral/.

Rodgers, Debra, Beth Calmes and Jonathan Grotts. "Creating National Standards from the Point of Care." *Nursing Administration Quarterly* 38, no. 1 (January/March 2014): 86-92.

Thomas, Emily. "Dying Man's Wish To Return To The Forest Comes True." *Huffington Post.* Accessed February 4, 2016. http://www.huffingtonpost.com/2014/06/15/dying-man-forest_n_5496691.html.

Thoreau, Henry David. *Walden.* Cambridge: University Press, 1910.

Tillich, Paul. *Theology of Culture* Oxford: Oxford University Press, 1964.

Turner, Victor. *Forest of Symbols.* Ithaca, NY: Cornell University Press, 1967.

————. "Symbols in African Ritual." *Science* 179, issue 4078 (16 Mar 1973): 1100. Accessed February 5, 2016, http://science.sciencemag.org/content/179/4078/1100.extract.

Underhill, Evelyn. *Practical Mysticism.* New York: E.P. Dutton & Company, 1915.

The United Methodist Book of Worship. Nashville: Abington Press, 1992.

van de Vijver, Fons J. R. "Emic-Etic Distinction." *Encyclopedia of Cross-Cultural School Psychology.* Accessed February 16, 2016. https://books.google.com/books?id=PaO3jsaGkeYC&pg=PA422&dq=emic+and+etic&hl=en&sa=X&ved=0ahUKEwjJ8cixtvfKAhUH7WMKHfuHAxYQ6AEIKzAC#v=onepage&q=emic%20and%20etic&f=false.

Williams-White, Sherry L. *Renewing Your Spirit: A Guide for Holidays and Special Days.* Louisville, KY: Hopeful Transitions, 2011.

Wolfelt, Alan. "Mourner's Bill of Rights." Center for Loss & Life Transition. Accessed February 14, 2015. http://www.centerforloss. com/2014/02/mourners-bill-rights/.

Wood, Nancy. *Many Winters: Prose and Poetry of the Pueblos.* New York: Doubleday Books for Young Readers, 1974.

"World Healing Prayers—Hindu." Accessed January 26, 2016. http:// www.worldhealingprayers.com/5.html.

Endnotes

1 "Many Americans Mix Multiple Faiths," Pew Research Center, accessed May 11, 2015, http://www.pewforum.org/2009/12/09/many-americans-mix-multiple-faiths/.

2 In this project, "the Spiritual" is used to denote a wide spectrum of existential experiences. The author attempted to use a noun to denote this experience in the widest sense. This term is explored more fully later in the book.

3 Peter Awn, *Comparative Mysticism*, ed. Steven Katz (Oxford: Oxford University Press, 2013), 249.

4 Robert J. Furey, *The Joy of Kindness* (New York: Crossroad, 1993), 138.

5 John Dewey, *A Common Faith* (New Haven: Yale University Press, 1934), 87.

6 Joseph Campbell, *Flight of the Wild Gander* (Novato, CA: New World Library, 2002), 143.

7 Paul Tillich, *Theology of Culture* (Oxford: Oxford University Press, 1964), 59.

8 Ibid., 54.

9 Louis-Marie Chauvet, *Symbol and Sacrament: A Sacramental Reinterpretation of Christian Existence*, trans. Patrick Madigan, SJ, and Madeleine Beaumont (Collegeville, MN: The Liturgical Press, 1995), 110.

10 Mircea Eliade, *Patterns in Comparative Religion*, trans. Rosemary Sheed (Lincoln, NE: First Bison Printing, 1996), 188-9.

11 Deborah Lipp, *The Elements of Ritual* (St. Paul: Llewellyn Publications, 2003), 9.

12 Mircea Eliade, *Images and Symbols: Studies in Religious Symbolism*, trans. Philip Mairet (Princeton, NJ: Princeton University Press, 1991), 177-8.

13 Chauvet, *Symbol and Sacrament*, 112.

14 Catherine Bell, *Ritual Theory, Ritual Practice* (New York: Oxford University Press, 2009), 184.

15 Victor Turner, *Forest of Symbols* (Ithaca, NY: Cornell University Press, 1967), 100.

16 Victor Turner, "Symbols in African Ritual," *Science* 179, issue 4078 (16 Mar 1973): 1100, accessed February 5, 2016, http://science.sciencemag.org/content/179/4078/1100.extract.

17 Bell, *Ritual Theory*, 187.

18 Jim Clarke, *Creating Rituals: A New Way of Healing for Everyday Life* (New York: Paulist Press, 2011), 6.

19 Eliade, *Patterns in Comparative Religion*, 456.

20 Nanette Asimov, "Stanford Gets a Chaplain for Atheists," *San Francisco Gate*, December 12, 2012, accessed November 22, 2014, http://www.sfgate.com/news/article/Stanford-gets-a-chaplain-for-atheists-4139991.php.

21 Megan McKenna and Tony Cowan, *Keepers of the Story* (Maryknoll, NY: Orbis Books, 1997), 64.

22 1 Corinthians 11:23b-25, (NRSV).

23 Miriam-Webster Dictionary, "Awareness," accessed May 11, 2015, cited in http://en.wikipedia.org/wiki/Awareness.

24 Jon Kabat-Zinn, *Coming to Our Senses: Healing Ourselves and the World through Mindfulness* (New York: Hyperion Books, 2005), 8.

25 Kenneth Krammer, *The Sacred Art of Dying* (New York: Paulist Press, 1988), 37.

26 Ibid., 38-9.

27 Ibid., 40.

28 Ibid., 50-3.

29 Ibid., 122.

30 Ibid., 135.

31 Ibid., 159-61.

32 Ibid., 163.

33 Ibid., 164.

34 "Pagan Rituals," Friends Alternative Funerals, accessed May 11, 2015, http://www.friendsaf.com/pagan-rituals/.

35 Eliade, *Patterns in Comparative Religion*, 216.

36 Scott Cunningham, *Earth, Air, Fire & Water* (St. Paul: Llewellyn Publications, 1999), 196-7.

37 Nan Merrill, *Psalms for Praying* (New York: Continuum International Publishing, 1996), 40.

38 "Sing Your Prayers: An Interview With Bobby McFerrin," *Huffington Post*, Healthy Living, last modified August 11, 2012, accessed November 22, 2014, http://www.huffingtonpost.com/omega-institute-for-holistic-studies/bobby-mcferrin_b_1582043.html.

39 John O'Donohue, *To Bless The Space Between Us* (New York: Doubleday, 2008).

40 Linda A. Gerdner, "Use of Individualized Music by Trained Staff and Family: Translating Research into Practice," *Journal of Gerontological Nursing* 31, no. 6 (June 2005): 22-30.

41 Emily Thomas, "Dying Man's Wish To Return To The Forest Comes True," *Huffington Post*, accessed February 4, 2016, http://www.huffingtonpost.com/2014/06/15/dying-man-forest_n_5496691.html.

42 "The *Ghusl* Procedure (Washing and Shrouding)," Muslim Funeral Services Ltd., accessed May 11, 2015, http://www.mfs.asn.au/ghusl--burial-steps.html.

43 Kate Braestrup, *Here If You Need Me* (New York: Back Bay Books, 2007), 29.

44 Martha R. Jacobs, *A Clergy Guide to End-of-Life Issues* (Cleveland, OH; The Pilgrim Press, 2010), 37-9.

45 William Shakespeare, *Hamlet*, act 5, scene 2.

46 James E. Miller, *When Mourning Dawns: Living Your Way Fully Through the Seasons of Your Grief—The DVD* (Fort Wayne, IN: Willowgreen, Inc., 2000).

47 Rachel Naomi Remen, *Kitchen Table Wisdom* (New York: Riverhead Books, 1996), 151-2.

48 Jerry R. O'Neill, *Peach, Limestone, and Green* (Bloomington, IN: West Bow Press, 2015), 95.

49 O'Donohue, *To Bless the Space*, 45.

50 Alan Wolfelt, "Mourner's Bill of Rights," Center for Loss & Life Transition, accessed February 14, 2015, http://www.centerforloss.com/2014/02/mourners-bill-rights/.

51 Fons J. R. van de Vijver, "Emic-Etic Distinction," *Encyclopedia of Cross-Cultural School Psychology*, accessed February 16, 2016, https://books.google.com/books?id=PaO3jsaGkeYC&pg=PA422&dq=emic+and+etic&hl=en&sa=X&ved=0ahUKEwjJ8cixtvfKAhUH7WMKHfuHAxYQ6AEIKzAC#v=onepage&q=emic%20and%20etic&f=false.

52 Evelyn Underhill, *Practical Mysticism* (New York: E.P. Dutton & Company, 1915), 151.

53 O'Donohue, *To Bless the Space*, 178.

54 Ibid., 170.

55 Ibid., 45.

56 W. H. Auden, *Selected Poems*, ed. Edward Mendelson, expanded 2nd ed. (New York: Vintage Books, 2007), 48.

57 Max Ehrmann, *Desiderata* (Wayland, MA: Bell & Son, 1927).

58 "Funeral Poetry," Natural Endings, accessed January 25, 2016, http://www.naturalendings.co.uk/funeral-poetry/.

59 "Uplifting Prayers—Serenity Prayer," Beliefnet, accessed January 26, 2016, http://www.beliefnet.com/Prayers/Protestant/Addiction/Serenity-Prayer.aspx.

60 Funeral Helper, "Remember Me," accessed January 25, 2016, http://funeral-helper.org/remember-me-in-your-heart-unknown-remembrance.html.

61 Henry David Thoreau, *Walden* (Cambridge: University Press, 1910), 118.

62 "Readings for a Funeral," Reverend Blue Sky, accessed February 15, 2016, https://revbluesky.wordpress.com/readings/readings-for-a-funeral/.

63 "Funeral Poetry."

64 Michael Leunig, *A Common Prayer* (North Blackburn, Victoria, Australia: Collins Dove, 1990), no page numbers.

65 Hafiz, *The Subject Tonight is Love: 60 Wild and Sweet Poems of Hafiz,* trans. by Daniel Ladinsky (New York: Penguin Compass, 1996), 50.

66 Jane Kenyon, *Collected Poems* (St. Paul: Graywolf Press, 2005), 213.

67 "Islamic Prayers for the Dying," A Good Dying, accessed January 26, 2016, http://www.a-good-dying.com/islamic-prayers.html.

68 Anne Morrow Lindbergh, *The Unicorn and Other Poems* (New York: Pantheon Books, 1956), 26.

69 "Grief Never Ends," Inspiration Online, accessed February 15, 2016, http://inspirationonline.com/2014/03/grief-never-ends/.

70 "Prayer & Spirituality," Holistic-Online.com, accessed November 22, 2014, http://1stholistic.com/spl_prayers/prayer_prayer-at-the-death-of-loved-one. htm.

71 *Occasional Services: A Companion to the Lutheran Book of Worship* (Minneapolis: Augsburg Publishing House, 1997),92-3.

72 *The United Methodist Book of Worship* (Nashville: Abington Press, 1992), 166.

73 Thich Nhat Hanh, *Plum Village Chanting and Recitation Book* (Berkeley, CA: Parallax Press, 2000), 182.

74 "World Healing Prayers—Hindu," accessed January 26, 2016, http://www. worldhealingprayers.com/5.html.

75 Ibid.

76 Judith C. Joseph, *Responding with Compassion* (Newtown PA: JCJoseph, Ltd., 2008), 96.

77 "My Jewish Learning," accessed January 26, 2016, http://www.myjewishlearning. com/texts/Liturgy_and_Prayers/Siddur_Prayer_Book/Torah_Service/Prayer_ for_the_Sick.shtml.

78 Deuteronomy 6:4.

79 "Uplifting Prayers—El Maley Rachamim," Beliefnet, accessed February 15, 2016, http://www.beliefnet.com/Prayers/Judaism/Death/El-Maley-Rachamim. aspx?q=Shine.

80 Mary Austin, *The American Rhythm* (Santa Fe: Sunstone Press, 2003), 125.

81 A Good Dying, "Pagan and Wiccan Prayers for the Dying," accessed January 26, 2016, http://www.a-good-dying.com/wiccan-prayers.html.

82 Joseph, *Responding,* 104.

83 Psalm 23, *New King James Version.* This translation is the one that is most familiar to many people.

84 Merrill, *Psalms.*

85 Psalm 91:1-2, 9-16 (NRSV).

86 Merrill, *Psalms,* 190-91.

87 Psalm 121, (NRSV).

88 Merrill, *Psalms,* 269.

89 Debra Rodgers, Beth Calmes and Jonathan Grotts, "Creating National Standards from the Point of Care," *Nursing Administration Quarterly* 38, no. 1 (January/ March 2014): 87. Whidbey General Hospital Palliative Care Team has adapted this ritual as printed here.

90 Sherry L. Williams-White, *Renewing Your Spirit: A Guide for Holidays and Special Days* (Louisville, KY: Hopeful Transitions, 2011) 56. This version is slightly adapted from the original.

Made in the USA
Lexington, KY
02 June 2017